Cartoonists

Other Books in the History Makers Series:

Cartoonists

History MAKERS

Cartoonists

By Bradley Steffens and Robyn M. Weaver

Lucent Books
P.O. Box 289011, San Diego, CA 92198-9011

Library of Congress Cataloging-in-Publication Data

Steffens, Bradley and Weaver, Robyn.
    Cartoonists / by Bradley Steffens and Robyn Weaver
        p.   cm. — (History makers)
    Includes bibliographical references and index.
    Summary: Discusses the lives and achievements of six cartoonists
who have made a major impact on society through their art and wit:
Chuck Jones, Charles Schulz, Garry Trudeau, Cathy Guisewite,
Matt Groening, and Scott Adams.
    ISBN 1-56006-668-7 (lib. : alk. paper)
    1. Comic books, strips, etc.—United States—History and criticism
Juvenile literature.   2. Cartoonists—United States Biography
Juvenile literature.   [1. Cartoonists.   2. Comic books, strips,
etc.—History and criticism.]   I. Title.   II. Series.
PN6725.W43   2000
741.5'092'273—dc21
[B]   99-41317
                                                                CIP

Cover photos: Cathy Guisewite (center), Chuck Jones (top right), Charles
Schulz (bottom right), Garry Trudeau (bottom left), Matt Groening (top left)

Copyright 2000 by Lucent Books, Inc.
P.O. Box 289011, San Diego, California 92198-9011

Printed in the U.S.A.

CONTENTS

FOREWORD

The literary form most often referred to as "multiple biography" was perfected in the first century A.D. by Plutarch, a perceptive and talented moralist and historian who hailed from the small town of Chaeronea in central Greece. His most famous work, *Parallel Lives*, consists of a long series of biographies of noteworthy ancient Greek and Roman statesmen and military leaders. Frequently, Plutarch compares a famous Greek to a famous Roman, pointing out similarities in personality and achievements. These expertly constructed and very readable tracts provided later historians and others, including playwrights like Shakespeare, with priceless information about prominent ancient personages and also inspired new generations of writers to tackle the multiple biography genre.

The Lucent History Makers series proudly carries on the venerable tradition handed down from Plutarch. Each volume in the series consists of a set of five to eight biographies of important and influential historical figures who were linked together by a common factor. In *Rulers of Ancient Rome*, for example, all the figures were generals, consuls, or emperors of either the Roman Republic or Empire; while the subjects of *Fighters Against American Slavery*, though they lived in different places and times, all shared the same goal, namely the eradication of human servitude. Mindful that politicians and military leaders are not (and never have been) the only people who shape the course of history, the editors of the series have also included representatives from a wide range of endeavors, including scientists, artists, writers, philosophers, religious leaders, and sports figures.

Each book is intended to give a range of figures—some well known, others less known; some who made a great impact on history, others who made only a small impact. For instance, by making Columbus's initial voyage possible, Spain's Queen Isabella I, featured in *Women Leaders of Nations*, helped to open up the New World to exploration and exploitation by the European powers. Unarguably, therefore, she made a major contribution to a series of events that had momentous consequences for the entire world. By contrast, Catherine II, the eighteenth-century Russian queen, and Golda Meir, the modern Israeli prime minister, did not play roles of global impact; however, their policies and actions significantly influenced the historical development of both their own countries and their regional neighbors. Regardless of their relative importance in the greater historical scheme, all of the figures chronicled in the History Makers series made contributions to posterity; and their public achievements, as well as what is known about their private lives, are presented and evaluated in light of the most recent scholarship.

In addition, each volume in the series is documented and substantiated by a wide array of primary and secondary source quotations. The primary source quotes enliven the text by presenting eyewitness views of the times and culture in which each history maker lived; while the secondary source quotes, taken from the works of respected modern scholars, offer expert elaboration and/ or critical commentary. Each quote is footnoted, demonstrating to the reader exactly where biographers find their information. The footnotes also provide the reader with the means of conducting additional research. Finally, to further guide and illuminate readers, each volume in the series features photographs, two bibliographies, and a comprehensive index.

The History Makers series provides both students engaged in research and more casual readers with informative, enlightening, and entertaining overviews of individuals from a variety of circumstances, professions, and backgrounds. No doubt all of them, whether loved or hated, benevolent or cruel, constructive or destructive, will remain endlessly fascinating to each new generation seeking to identify the forces that shaped their world.

Popular Art

Cartoons are everywhere. They appear in almost every medium of communication—newspapers, magazines, books, television, motion pictures, videos, websites, trading cards, greeting cards, stickers, posters, and more. Cartoons decorate watches, backpacks, mugs, plates, key chains, even golf clubs—virtually any item that can be printed on or molded into a recognizable shape. Cartoons

are painted on walls, light up in scoreboards, and decorate aerial blimps. Cartoons are even drawn into human skin by tattoo artists.

The only media in which cartoons do not appear are radio, sound recordings, and live theater. These exceptions are obvious but are worth noting because they identify the most important feature of cartoons: They are pictorial. Cartoons often include words, but they do not have to. Animated cartoons usually include voices and music, but they can also be silent. Regardless of the medium, however, a cartoon must include a picture.

A giant balloon in the shape of the cartoon character Snoopy floats down the street during Macy's Thanksgiving Day parade.

Most cartoons appear on the "funny pages" of the newspaper, but they are not always funny. Adventure, action, romance, and fantasy are all portrayed in cartoons, especially in comic books. Cartoons make readers laugh, but they can also make them think, become angry, or even cry. Drawing on the full range of human experience and evoking every possible emotion, cartoonists are artists in the fullest sense of the word.

The cartoonists in this book have not only entertained their audiences but have also influenced other artists in their field. Charles Schulz transformed the humorous, or gag, comic strip with his unique blending of visual and verbal wit. Chuck Jones and his colleagues at Warner Brothers Studios created a cast of characters and a fast-paced visual style that set the standard for generations of animators. Garry Trudeau showed that comic strips can add to the political and social debate as much as political cartoons do. Cathy Guisewite proved that a highly personal comic focused on the travails of a single woman can appeal to a broad range of readers. Matt Groening demonstrated that an intelligent animated program aimed at adults can succeed in prime-time television. And Scott Adams revealed the workplace as fertile ground for satire.

Each of these cartoonists has influenced popular culture as well. The world would be a different place without Charlie Brown and Snoopy, Road Runner and Wile E. Coyote, Michael Doonesbury and Zonker Harris, Cathy, the Simpsons, and Dilbert, just to name a few of the cultural icons created by these cartoonists. Like other satirists and commentators on the social scene, these cartoonists have shaped attitudes toward a wide range of personal, moral, political, and cultural issues. Mostly, though, they have entertained, giving their fans one thing that is always in short supply—a chance for a good laugh.

CHAPTER 1

The History of Cartooning

The modern-day cartoon has its origins in illustrated books of the Middle Ages. Most of the books produced in Europe during this time were Christian scriptures and religious texts. These works were copied by hand by monks who worked in scriptoriums, the writing rooms of Christian monasteries. Because they were hand-written, these books are known as manuscripts, derived from the Latin words *manus*, which means "hand," and *scribere*, which means "to write."

The monks who created these books often used pictures to il-lustrate the text. Sometimes the monks enlarged the initial letter of a section of text and drew tiny pictures, or miniatures, within the outlines of the letter. They also decorated the pages with colorful borders. Patterns of entwined vines and flowers blossomed around the text. Birds, animals, and imaginary beasts peered out from the foliage. These and other pictures inserted into the text helped tell the stories of biblical figures and Christian saints.

To make the pictures easy to understand, the monks often used exaggeration in their drawing. Sweeping gestures and vivid ex-pressions helped clarify the action. Doves and angels hovered near the holy figures, while imps and demons waited on the evil ones. The pictures not only helped explain the text but evoked feelings of their own—wonder, fear, sometimes even terror. Cartoonist Syd Hoff and others believe that these early illustrations were similar to cartoons. As Hoff explains,

> During the Middle Ages, cartoons and caricatures often dealt with Death and the Devil, as evidenced in prayer-books and places of worship. . . . Of course, these car-toonists and caricaturists were pandering to the most backward notions of the wicked and superstitious, but in that they brought with them skilled drawing and a high grade of satire.[1]

The invention of the printing press in 1455 made it unnecessary to copy manuscripts by hand, but that did not mean the end of book illustration. On the contrary, the printing press created a greater need for book illustration than ever before. Thousands of books and pamphlets were printed in the fifteenth and sixteenth centuries, and many were illustrated with woodcuts and engravings. Unlike the manuscripts of the Middle Ages, printed books covered a wide variety of subjects, not just religion.

The printing press made it possible to publish information quickly. Printers began to publish letters and accounts of important events on single-page sheets known as news books. Probably the most important news book of the fifteenth century came from the court of King Ferdinand and Queen Isabella of Spain. Published in April 1493, it described the successful voyage of an Italian sailor named Christopher Columbus.

News books covered single events, but in January 1609, two new publications that described several current events appeared. One was published by Johann Carolus in Strasbourg, France, and the other was published by Lucas Schulte in Wolfenbüttel, Germany. Soon printers all across Europe began to copy Carolus's and Schulte's idea of regularly published newspapers. By 1621, weekly newspapers were being printed in Basel, Vienna, Frankfurt, Hamburg, Berlin, Antwerp, Amsterdam, and London. These news

A woodcut from the Cologne Bible, printed in 1479, depicts a scene from the Book of Revelation. Such simple, exaggerated drawings are the forerunners of modern-day cartoons.

books and early newspapers often contained illustrations of the events described in their pages. They also contained the first modern cartoons: single-panel drawings that illustrated not an actual event but an imagined scene or idea.

By the eighteenth century, political and social issues became targets of humorous drawings. One of the most popular American cartoonists of this period was Benjamin Franklin (1706–1790). Franklin printed the *Pennsylvania Gazette* and often added his own artwork. His cartoons focused on political issues. Syd Hoff considers Franklin one of the most important American cartoonists:

> Benjamin Franklin is undoubtedly the father of American political cartooning. At the outbreak of the French and Indian War, the celebrated printer, publisher, author, and editor . . . conceived this figure of a snake, cut into as many parts as there were colonies, that became familiar to thousands of readers of newspapers and handbills. Even if a cut-up snake can't come back to life, Franklin's cartoon did, reappearing in 1765 at the time of the Stamp Act, and again in 1776 when the colonies revolted.[2]

Although Franklin drew many cartoons and caricatures, the cut-up snake has remained the one most often associated with his cartooning history.

Benjamin Franklin drew this cartoon of a cut-up snake to promote a union of American colonies.

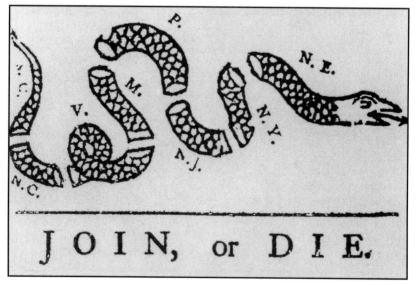

Because of its open elections and constitutionally guaranteed freedom of the press, the United States provided fertile soil for cartoonists, especially political cartoonists. At this time—long before radio, television, and the Internet—most people learned about events through the newspapers. As a result, newspaper cartoonists enjoyed even more clout than they do today.

One of the most important political cartoonists of the nineteenth century was Thomas Nast, who is remembered both for his cartoons and his illustrations. His cartoons helped shape the public opinion about many issues and elected officials, as biographer David Relin notes:

One of the most influential political cartoonists of his time, Thomas Nast also created a widely popular likeness of Santa Claus.

> Nast's pen helped to make and break careers of presidents and powerful politicians—and even rallied the nation to war. Nast's cartoons—many of them published in the magazine *Harper's Weekly*—were eagerly anticipated by hundreds of thousands of Americans. In an era long before CNN, the public tuned in to each Nast Cartoon to get an up-to-date picture of the nation's political news. Many of the images he helped popularize—including the Democratic donkey, the Republican elephant, Uncle Sam, and Santa Claus—are still at the center of American culture today.[3]

Nast's power and influence inspired other cartoonists to not only entertain but help focus public attention on society's problems. During the late 1800s, cartoonists attacked unfair labor laws, crooked politicians, and even the Spanish-American War.

The Comic Strip

Up till and throughout the nineteenth century, virtually all cartoons were single-panel drawings. Each cartoon was self-contained, not part of a series. Characters might reappear in the work of a cartoonist from time to time, but the cartoons did not tell any kind of story. Toward the end of the nineteenth century, this began to change.

At the time, it was common for cartoonists to illustrate novels that appeared in installments in the newspaper. Readers looked forward not just to reading the ongoing story but to seeing the drawings of the characters day after day. According to cartoonist Robert Harvey, these illustrated novel installments led to the development of the comic strip:

> Today's comic strip is the lineal descendent of the nineteenth century humorous drawings that accompanied the serial publication of novels . . . and that appeared in newspapers and other periodicals. . . . Toward the end of the century, great metropolitan newspapers battled for readers, and, in the attempt to attract readers and build circulation, they began publishing extravagant Sunday supplements.[4]

Cartoonists began to string panels together into a short sequence of panels, or comic strip. The strip allowed the cartoonist to set up a joke with two or three panels before providing the punch line. The strip also allowed the cartoonist to introduce more characters without cluttering the picture or confusing the reader. To make it clear which character was speaking, cartoonists put each character's words inside a circle known as a speech balloon. The "tail" of the speech balloon pointed toward the character who was speaking. According to Robert C. Harvey, speech balloons transformed the art of cartooning:

> Speech balloons breathe into comic strips their peculiar life. In all other graphic representations, characters are doomed to wordless posturing and pantomime—but in comic strips, they speak. . . .Thus, the inclusion of speech balloons within the pictures gives the words and pictures concurrence—the lifelike illusion that the characters we see are speaking even as we see them.[5]

Speech balloons enhanced the cartoonist's ability to tell complete stories. Each strip related a brief episode, and cartoonists also began to carry the story over from one day to the next, just as the serialized novels did.

Color

Until 1895 most comic strips and cartoons were black-ink drawings printed in newspapers and magazines. When the four-color rotary press was invented, the first splash of color was added to a comic strip character drawn by Richard Outcault in his strip *Hogan's Alley*. On February 17, 1895, a new color press printed the boy's shirt in yellow. The "Yellow Kid" was a sensation and soon became a regular feature of New York's *Sunday World* newspaper supplement.

Readership Wars

With the help of the Yellow Kid, sales of the *Sunday World* surged. William Randolph Hearst, the owner of the rival *Morning Journal*, became so concerned with the Yellow Kid's success that he hired Outcault to work for the *Morning Journal* instead. To counter Hearst's move, Joseph Pulitzer, the publisher of the *World*, hired another artist to continue drawing the Yellow Kid for his newspaper. Spectators watching Hearst and Pulitzer use the Yellow Kid to fight for readers dubbed the newspapers "yellow

In 1895 Joseph Pulitzer's Sunday World *printed the big-eared kid in Richard Outcault's* Hogan's Alley *with yellow ink. The first color cartoon character, the Yellow Kid became a sensation.*

journals." Later the term *yellow journalism* would be used to indicate the type of sensationalized news stories published by these and other newspapers of the era.

The fact that major newspapers fought over a cartoon character reveals how popular the comics had become. To gain more readers, newspapers printed all the comics on the same page, known as the funny page.

> Beginning with the Yellow Kid, the comics enjoyed a prized position in newspapering. They sold papers. And that was a vital consideration in the industry at the time. . . . Newspapers began to be wrapped in the comics section. The funnies advertised the Sunday edition. . . . And they served this unique function in most cities for most of the century.[6]

Reflecting America

Many early comic strips sought only to entertain, often reflecting popular humor and lifestyles of the time. One of the first successful comic strips, *Mutt and Jeff*, created by Bud Fisher, portrayed two ordinary men who lived ordinary lives. Bud Fisher began the strip on November 15, 1907, with Mutt's first appearance. First named *A. Mutt*, the strip emphasized Mutt's schemes for earning a fast dollar. Later his friend Jeff, who had even less intelligence than Mutt (short for mutton head), was added. The strip humorously reflected the desire of poor and middle-class people to get ahead and the problems they encountered when they let their desire for money overrule their common sense.

Strips telling continuous stories became popular between the 1920s and 1930s. Some reflected family life, such as Harold Gray's *Little Orphan Annie*. Others focused on the adventures of dashing heroes and heroines. These strips were fast paced and had a suspenseful climax in the last panel instead of a joke as in humorous strips.

One of the most influential adventure cartoonists was Roy Crane. His first strip, *Wash Tubbs*, became popular when Crane sent Wash to the South Seas. For that adventure, Crane introduced a new character named Captain Easy. Easy was so loved by readers that Crane gave him his own strip. One cartoonist said that Captain Easy was the first comic book adventure hero:

> It is almost impossible to overestimate the impact of this character on those who wrote and drew adventure stories

Hank Ketchum, the creator of Dennis the Menace, *one of the many gag cartoons that became popular in the 1950s, meets with six-year-old actor Jay North, who played the character on television.*

in comic strips and comic books in the thirties. Cartoonist Gil Kane, who began his comic book career in the early forties, once chanted a litany of credit to Crane before an audience at the San Diego Comic Convention: "Superman was Captain Easy," he said, "Batman was Easy." And he listed several more characters before he stopped.[7]

The Rise of Wise Guys

The popularity of the adventure strips began to wane at about the same time that the television became a staple in American homes.

Some historians believe that the advent of television made the comic strip adventures seem less exciting. Others believe that adventures were squeezed off the funny page by the rise of humorous strips such as Mort Walker's *Beetle Bailey* and Charles Schulz's *Peanuts*, both of which debuted in 1950.

Although their drawing styles were very different, Walker and Schulz both used an unexpected twist, or non sequitur, in the final panel to create humor in their strips. In *Peanuts*, the non sequitur usually occurred when the children in the strip suddenly spoke like adults. In *Beetle Bailey*, the non sequitur often was more visual. Sometimes the main character, Beetle Bailey, a private in the army, would find an unexpected way to escape from work. The surprise endings in these strips caused readers to smile, chuckle, and sometimes laugh.

Peanuts and *Beetle Bailey* soared in popularity. Soon other cartoonists were copying the non sequitur–style strips. Johnny Hart's *B.C.*, Tom Ryan's *Tumbleweeds*, Russell Myers's *Broom-Hilda*, Chris Browne's *Hagar the Horrible*, and Jim Davis's *Garfield* all succeeded by using the non sequitur approach. It wasn't long before funny comics took over the funny pages, pushing aside all but a handful of adventure cartoons.

Peanuts *creator Charles Schulz poses with toys based on characters in his comic strip.*

Off the Pages and into the Home

Some of the characters in humorous cartoons became so popular that entrepreneurs began to put their likenesses on a variety of household items. Merchandising, selling a company the rights to put a cartoon character's likeness on its products, has become big business. Charles Schulz's lovable beagle, Snoopy, was one of the first cartoon characters to be successfully merchandised. By 1990, Snoopy had made a great deal of money for his creator:

He's one of the biggest money-makers in show biz, and he's helped his creator become the 10th-highest-paid artist in American entertainment. His name is Snoopy, and he's the most popular comic-strip character in the world. Last year the big-nosed beagle with recurring dreams of glory enabled Charles Schulz to earn $28 million.[8]

Because of Schulz's success, many other cartoonists have taken the plunge into merchandising ventures. Jim Davis and his cat Garfield earned $11 million in 1990. Garry Trudeau's *Doonesbury* and Bill Watterson's *Calvin and Hobbes* have both earned multiple millions of dollars.

The explosion of merchandising and the advent of electronic technologies such as video games and the Internet have propelled cartoons into the forefront of American entertainment. Even with modern technology and changing markets for their work, cartoonists remain true to their core goal. They continue to look at the world around them in a slightly warped way to find humor in everyday situations and share it with their readers.

CHAPTER 2

Charles Schulz

Starting in October 1999, United Media began a yearlong celebration commemorating the fiftieth anniversary of its most successful comic strip, *Peanuts*. Since it debuted on October 2, 1950, the daily comic featuring "Good Ol' Charlie Brown" and his many friends and acquaintances grew into the most successful comic strip in history. In September 1999, United Media reported that *Peanuts* was carried by twenty-six hundred newspapers worldwide, reaching an estimated 355 million readers in seventy-five countries. Translated

into twenty-one different languages, *Peanuts* was read by at least 55 million people each day. Hundreds of millions more watched the many television specials and commercials featuring characters from the strip. Worldwide retail sales from publishing, television, and product licensing of *Peanuts* characters exceeded $1 billion a year.

Despite the vast wealth his strip brought him—or perhaps because of it—Charles Schulz, the creator of *Peanuts*, lives simply. For fifty years he followed the same routine almost every day. Around 7:30 A.M., he took a short walk to the ice rink he owns, sat down in the snack bar, had coffee, and read the newspaper. Around 9:00 A.M., he took another short walk to his art studio, answered his mail, settled behind his drawing table, and worked on the comic. Although he could easily have afforded to hire assistants, he did not. He was the sole creator of the pen-and-ink world of the children and animals known as the *Peanuts* gang.

Charles Schulz at work in his studio.

22

Born to Draw a Comic Strip

Charles Schulz sold his first magazine cartoon—a drawing of a small child sitting at the end of a chaise lounge reading a book with his feet propped up on an ottoman—to the *Saturday Evening Post* in 1948. Schulz was just twenty-six years old at the time, but he had already been drawing cartoons for many years. Like many cartoonists, Schulz had started experimenting with his craft as a child. He later recalled that he had decided on his career at an early age:

It seems beyond the comprehension of people that someone can be born to draw comic strips, but I think I was. My ambition from earliest memory was to produce a daily comic strip.[9]

Whether or not he was "born to draw," Charles Monroe Schulz was certainly born into a family that prized comics beyond the norm. Schulz's father, Carl, a barber, routinely bought four different Sunday newspapers just to keep up with the different strips each carried. Carl was so eager to read the funnies that he ventured into downtown St. Paul, Minnesota, where the Schulzes lived, on Saturday nights to pick up the first available copies of the Sunday papers. Sometimes Charles accompanied his father on these Saturday night trips. He later told a biographer that he vividly recalls standing outside the *Saint Paul Pioneer Press* building, peering through the windows, watching the comic pages roll off the newspaper's giant rotary presses.

Carl Schulz was not the only grown-up fan of the comics in the family. One of Charles's cousins was nicknamed Corky after a baby in the comic strip *Gasoline Alley*. Two days after Charles Schulz was born on November 26, 1922, an uncle nicknamed him Sparky after a racehorse named Spark Plug, also in *Gasoline Alley*. Amazingly, the offbeat nickname stuck. Today Charles Schulz's friends and family still call him Sparky.

Like most young children, Charles Schulz experimented with drawing. Unlike most children, however, Schulz showed talent. Not only was he able to draw recognizable objects, but he also combined them in creative ways. In kindergarten, for example, he drew a man shoveling snow beside a palm tree. Schulz's teacher was so impressed with the unusual drawing that she told her young student, "Someday, Charles, you are going to be an artist."[10]

Not surprisingly, the young Charles Schulz used his drawing skills to copy images from the comics his father loved. Schulz's ability to produce exact copies of popular cartoon characters impressed not only his parents but also his peers: "When I was a kid, I drew Mickey Mouse and Popeye and people were always asking me to draw. Kids asked me to draw Popeye on the covers of their notebooks."[11]

Schulz was an outstanding student in elementary school, skipping two half-grades. By high school, however, he had become self-conscious about being a year younger than the other students. The teenage Schulz was tall, skinny, and wracked with the insecurity that would become the hallmark of his most famous character, Charlie Brown. Schulz also was going through difficult times at home. His mother, Dena, had cancer. Schulz's teenage years passed sadly as the young man watched his mother slowly dying.

Charles Schulz as a senior in high school.

Schulz became disinterested in his studies during his high school years, but he poured more of his energy into his drawing. A high school art teacher encouraged him to submit his cartoons to the annual yearbook, but the effort was fruitless. "I waited and waited for the annual to come out," Schulz later recalled. "When it did, my drawings were not in it."[12] No one ever explained to Schulz why his work was not included in the yearbook, and the sensitive young man never asked.

About the same time that the yearbook editors were rejecting Schulz's work, his mother noticed a small advertisement in the newspaper for a correspondence art school. The ad asked, "Do you like to draw?" As she read these words, Dena immediately thought of her son. In one of the last but most important acts of her life, Dena showed the ad to her husband and son, suggesting that Charles apply to the school.

All three members of the Schulz family agreed that the art school was a good idea, but the Schulzes faced a major obstacle. Tuition for the course was $170. In 1939, this was a great deal of money. The nation was still in the grips of the worst economic depression in its history. Dena was not covered by any

Charles Schulz, second from right in the top row, poses with other members of his high school art club. Schulz submitted cartoons to the high school yearbook but they were not used.

health insurance, so all of her medical bills had to be paid out of pocket. And Carl earned just 35 cents for each haircut he gave in the barber shop he owned. The art school's tuition represented more than four hundred haircuts—at least a month's worth of work. In light of these hardships, Carl and Dena Schulz's decision to enroll Charles in art school speaks volumes about their belief in their seventeen-year-old son.

He would not disappoint them.

Success was not immediate, however. The art school course consisted of twelve divisions. Schulz excelled at some but proved average in others. For example, he received a grade of C-plus in Division Five, "Drawing of Children," a surprisingly low grade for a man who would later achieve worldwide renown for a comic strip filled with children.

Growing and Grieving

About the same time Schulz finished the art courses, he was drafted into the army to serve in World War II. Shortly after he reported for duty, his mother died. It was at this time that Schulz began to experience chronic depression. He also began to have panic attacks when confronted with uncomfortable situations such as public places. The name of this condition is *agoraphobia*, from the Greek word meaning "fear of the marketplace." Some psychologists believe that a tendency toward agoraphobia, like other mental disorders, may be inherited. Schulz believes his father was agoraphobic. "He used his work, the barbershop, as a reason never to travel or do anything," Schulz remembered. "He never went anywhere by himself, either. Even when he went fishing there had to be someone else along. He would never have guessed what he was feeling had a name, but I'm convinced that's what it was."[13]

Schulz has openly discussed his psychological problems. In his book *You Don't Look 35, Charlie Brown!* Schulz wrote:

> There must be different kinds of loneliness, or at least different degrees of loneliness, but the most terrifying loneliness is not experienced by everyone and can be understood by only a few. I compare the panic in this kind of loneliness to the dog we see running frantically down the road pursuing the family car. He is not really being left behind, for the family knows it is to return, but for that moment in his limited understanding, he is being left alone forever, and he has to run and run to survive.[14]

Although a person may inherit a tendency toward agoraphobia, that does not mean he or she will be afflicted by it. Usually, the disorder is triggered by a traumatic event of some kind. Biographer Rheta Grimsley Johnson believes that Schulz's agoraphobia was triggered by the stressful events he endured at the beginning of 1943:

> The origin of his fundamental sadness remains mostly a mystery to Schulz and to those around him. His mother's death from cancer when she was forty-eight and he was twenty certainly might have triggered it. Schulz carries that memory with him always, fingering its tragic components like a rosary. At the same time his mother died, Schulz was drafted to serve in World War II. Schulz made a good soldier, but the triple whammy of losing his mother, the security of home, and control of his life may have changed him forever. . . . Even today [Schulz] cannot discuss his mother or look at her photograph without becoming extremely emotional.[15]

The Start of a Career

In the army, Schulz again used his drawing skills to make friends. Before long, he was decorating the outside of his fellow soldiers' letters with cartoons. His drawings showed round-headed soldiers engaged in various aspects of barracks life—cleaning, marching, writing letters, opening packages from home. During his time in the army, Schulz served as an infantryman, a staff sergeant, and a leader of a machine-gun squad. In February 1945, Schulz's division was shipped overseas. He was stationed in France until April, when the division began to move. Schulz saw about five weeks of combat before the war in Europe came to a close. Many years later, Schulz would draw on his World War II experience in making the television special "What Have We Learned, Charlie Brown?" a program that recounts the Allied invasion of Normandy.

A 1966 photo shows the artist drawing his popular cartoon character, Charlie Brown.

After the war, Schulz returned to St. Paul determined to find a job as an artist. A small Roman Catholic magazine, *Timeless Topix*, hired Schulz on a freelance basis to do the lettering in the comic strips it published. Schulz also applied for a job at the Art Instruction School in Minneapolis, Minnesota, the same correspondence school he had enrolled in as a teenager. He was hired to correct the lessons the students mailed in.

At the Art Instruction School, Schulz met a young man named Charlie Brown. Although nothing like the round-headed boy Schulz would later draw, the real-life Charlie Brown did furnish Schulz with the name that would be linked to him forever. Another person Schulz met at the art school did inspire a *Peanuts* character. She was a pretty, red-haired woman named Donna Mae Johnson.

Early in 1950, Schulz and Johnson began to date. At the time, Johnson was also dating several other men. By June, Johnson had introduced Schulz to her family and the romance had blossomed. One of Johnson's other suitors, Al Wold, proposed to her in July. "It was a terrible thing, really, caring for two people like that," Johnson later recalled. "Up to the last minute it was the most difficult decision."[16] Finally, Johnson accepted Wold's proposal. Schulz was heartbroken. The pain of that heartbreak fueled hundreds of cartoons about Charlie Brown's crush on a little red-haired girl who scarcely knows he exists.

While working at the Art Instruction School, Schulz perfected the drawing style that would make him famous. In 1947, Schulz approached the *Saint Paul Pioneer Press* with the idea for a weekly comic featuring children. The editors decided to use the cartoon in what was then called the women's section of the paper. One Saturday night in 1947, the large rotary presses that Schulz had watched as a child applied the first impressions of his *Li'l Folks* to the pages of the *Saint Paul Pioneer Press*.

Robert C. Harvey, author of *The Art of the Funnies*, described the appeal of *Li'l Folks*:

> The feature ran once a week, a collection of single-panel cartoons about the antics of little children who seemed a bit more sophisticated than most cartoon children. The kids were cute because of the way Schulz drew them. They were all tiny, and Schulz distorted proportions—giving them round heads as big as their bodies—in a way that made them seem more diminutive. And tiny was cute.[17]

Peanuts

In the late 1940s, Schulz began to submit samples of *Li'l Folks* strips to newspaper syndicates, companies that provide material to large numbers of newspapers. In 1950, United Feature Syndicate expressed an interest in Schulz's work, so Schulz traveled to New York to meet with its executives. He showed the editors the single-panel *Li'l Folks* cartoons as well as samples of a strip he had tried. The syndicate preferred the strip, as did Schulz. The editors, however, did not like the name of Schulz's strip. They felt that *Li'l Folks* was too close to the popular strip *Li'l Abner*. They also thought it might be confused with a defunct comic named *Little Folks*. Schulz did not have another name in mind, so the committee began to brainstorm. One of those present, Bill Anderson, suggested *Peanuts*. Everyone liked the name, except for Schulz. He thought it made the strip sound insignificant. Unable to come up with an acceptable alternative, Schulz finally agreed to the name. Decades later, however, the famous cartoonist was still grousing over the naming incident:

> *Peanuts* is the worst title ever thought up for a comic strip....I don't even like the word. It's not a nice word. It's totally ridiculous, has no meaning, is simply confusing, and has no dignity. And I think my humor has dignity. The strip I was going to draw I thought would have dignity. The strip I was going to draw would have class. They didn't know when I walked in there that here was a fanatic. Here was a kid totally dedicated to what he was going to do. And then to label something that was going to be a life's work with a name like *Peanuts* was really insulting.[18]

The first *Peanuts* strip introduced "Good Ol' Charlie Brown." One by one, other characters made their way onto Schulz's tiny stage: Schroeder, the piano-playing lover of music; Violet, a neighbor girl; Lucy, the loudmouthed fussbudget; Linus, Lucy's philosophical younger brother; Snoopy, Charlie Brown's dog; and many more.

As in *Li'l Folks*, most of the humor in *Peanuts* comes from the unlikely, grown-up observations the children make about their world. In one early strip, Charlie Brown tells Violet that he has two candy bars and asks if she would like one. Like a typical small child, Violet does not want to share. "One isn't enough," she says as she reaches for the second bar. "I want both of them." Left without any candy, Charlie Brown does not cry. Instead, he remarks, "I admire frankness in a person."[19]

Part of the humor in *Peanuts* comes from the distinct personalities of each of the characters. Readers of the strip come to expect a certain reaction from each character, and they usually get it. The repetition can be funny. Robert C. Harvey considered the running gag to be one of Schulz's innovations:

> To the occasional reader of Peanuts, Charlie Brown's remarking "Good grief" at the end of a strip is not terribly funny; but for regular readers of the strip the simple phrase has taken on a significance of uproarious proportions. The running gag is hardly a new invention with Schulz, but he stretched it further than most comic strip artists had done previously.[20]

The strength of the characters allowed Schulz to develop another innovation, what he called the "slight incident."

> I can remember creating it sitting at the desk . . . what would happen in the three panels that I was drawing at that time was a very brief and slight incident. No one had ever done that before in comic strips.[21]

An example of the slight incident occurs in an early strip when Lucy ties Linus's shoes. "No that's too loose . . . I feel flimsy . . . ," Linus tells his sister in the first panel. "How's that?" Lucy asks in the second panel. "Too tight! Too tight! Aaugh," Linus screams. "All right, how's that?" Lucy asks in the third panel. "Whew! that's fine. Yes, that's fine! Whew!" says Linus. In the fourth panel Linus comments to Charlie Brown, "I can't even breathe if my shoelaces aren't tied just right."[22] The action in this episode—tying shoes—is mundane; the humor comes from Linus's reactions, his extreme sensitivity. This innovation also influenced Schulz's peers. "Once Schulz had demonstrated how singular personalities can generate humor in a strip," observed Robert Harvey, "other cartoonists began mining the same territory."[23]

Near Failure

The humor in *Peanuts* was more subtle than that of most comic strips of the time. As a result, the strip was not an instant success. Only seven newspapers carried the strip at first. Within three months, one of those papers canceled its subscription. In a reader's poll of comic strips taken by the *New York World Telegram*, *Peanuts* was ranked last. At the end of the strip's first year, only about twenty newspapers had subscribed. The syndicate needed at least one hundred subscribers to break even. Many people at the syndicate felt that the strip should be dropped.

To save the strip, sales manager Harry Gilburt devised a plan. Believing that the strip had introduced too many characters too quickly, Gilburt developed small ads introducing each of the characters in the strip. "The promotion expenses were great, but I thought the strip deserving," said Gilburt. "It had a spark, something almost indefinable."[24]

The ads seemed to help. They also bought Schulz time to find his comic style. "Fortunately for all of us, Peanuts suddenly took off—the rapid development of Schulz's talent in art and comic sense began to pay off," said Jim Freeman, the United Feature Syndicate editor who had first shown interest in Schulz's strip. "Our salesmen eventually didn't have to sell the strip. They merely took orders."[25]

Fans get a behind-the-scenes look at the creation of Peanuts *during the filming of "It's Your Twentieth Television Anniversary, Charlie Brown."*

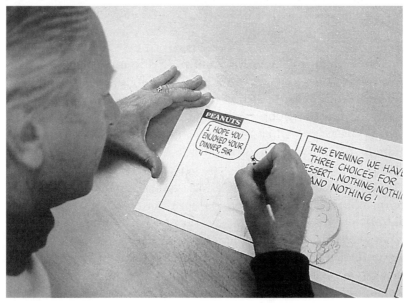

As his dream of being a cartoonist was coming true, Schulz met, dated, and then proposed to Joyce Halverson, the sister of a coworker at the Art Instruction School. The two got married in 1951 and started a family. The Schulzes moved to Colorado Springs, Colorado, for a brief time, then moved to Sebastopol, California. The family returned to Minnesota for six years before returning to California in 1958, where they remained. Together, Charles and Joyce Schulz had five children, Meredith, Charles Jr., Craig, Amy, and Jill.

Throughout the 1950s, subscriptions to *Peanuts* rose steadily. Schulz continued to refine the strip, further developing his characters, adding new ones, and dropping others. In 1962, Schulz collected some of the best aphorisms, or sayings, from the strip into a book entitled *Happiness Is a Warm Puppy*. It became an instant best-seller. Two years later, a Methodist minister named Robert L. Short wrote a book called *The Gospel According to Peanuts*, which discussed the religious content of Schulz's strip. In April 1965, *Time* magazine did a cover story on the *Peanuts* phenomenon. Later that same year, the first *Peanuts* television special, "A Charlie Brown Christmas," aired. For the first time, fans of the strip heard the voices of Charlie Brown, Linus, and Lucy. It was one of the highest-rated programs of the year. Schulz and the syndicate also began to license more and more products bearing the likenesses of the *Peanuts* characters.

With success came wealth beyond anything Schulz had imagined. Joyce Schulz helped her husband oversee the growing *Peanuts* empire, building the family home, the ice rink, and the business offices and sheltering the cartoonist from the flood of offers that poured in.

Success did not spoil *Peanuts*. Instead, it seemed to free Schulz to experiment more. In October 1965, Schulz had Snoopy don the helmet and scarf of a World War I flying ace, climb atop his doghouse, and fly off to battle Germany's Red Baron. With this flight of fancy, *Peanuts* soared to heights achieved by no comic strip before or since. Mort Walker, creator of the comic strip *Beetle Bailey*, looked on with dismay as Schulz again stretched the bounds of the comic strip world:

> When Charlie Schulz first did Snoopy in a helmet sitting on top of the dog house pretending he was fighting the Red Baron, I thought Schulz was going to ruin the strip. I could believe Snoopy sitting up there sort of pretending or imagining he was a vulture or something, but where did he get a helmet? What does a dog know about World War I or the Red Baron? And then he showed bullet holes in the dog house. I said, Good golly—this has gone beyond the pale. Then when it became so popular, I said, it just shows you—comics, as Rube Goldberg used to say, are an individual effort that is so beyond explaining that nobody could ever mastermind it.[26]

For the next thirty-five years, Schulz continued to experiment with a less verbal, more visual style. In 1972, he introduced Woodstock, a tiny yellow bird who became Snoopy's sidekick, which provided Schulz with the chance to create even more visual gags. Likewise, Schulz's creation of Spike, Snoopy's scruffy brother who lives in Needles, California, allowed him to create sight gags out of the desert landscape. In one memorable 1999 cartoon, Spike is dribbling a soccer ball toward a makeshift goal. Between Spike and the goal stands a saguaro cactus, its upraised arms suggesting just enough of the human form to make it serve as a goalie.

Schulz has received many awards for his work. The National Cartoonist Society has presented Schulz with the Reuben Award for Outstanding Cartoonist of the Year twice, in 1955 and 1964. In 1956 Schulz received the Yale Humor Award as Outstanding Humorist of the Year. In 1960 he was recognized for the more serious content of his strip by the National Education Society, which presented him with the School Bell Award. In 1978 he was named International Cartoonist of the Year.

Together with Lee Mendelson, his friend and creative partner, Schulz has created more than thirty animated television specials, which have been nominated for twenty-seven Emmy awards and have won five. Schulz and Mendelson have also won two Peabody Awards for outstanding achievements in television programming.

A plush Snoopy doll appears to review Schulz's work in a scene from "It's Your Twentieth Television Anniversary, Charlie Brown."

In 1983, they created a Saturday morning cartoon show, *The Charlie Brown and Snoopy Show*, which ran for three seasons.

Animation allows Schulz to try things not possible in a four-panel comic strip—both visually and dramatically. He and Mendelson have used the animated format to educate and inspire as well as entertain. In addition to "What Have We Learned, Charlie Brown?" which recounts the events of World War II, Schulz and Mendelson created *This Is America, Charlie Brown*, an animated miniseries that explores U.S. history. Drawing on his own family's encounter with cancer, Schulz created a special entitled "Why, Charlie Brown, Why?" In the program, Linus's friend Janice is diagnosed with leukemia, cancer of the bone marrow. She suffers through the nausea and hair loss caused by chemotherapy and struggles with the feeling of not fitting in with the kids at school. Through it all, Linus sticks by his friend. Critics applauded Schulz for honestly addressing the details of cancer without losing his sense of humor.

In describing the spirit that drove him to continue his work over so many years, Schulz once said:

Why do musicians compose symphonies and poets write poems? They do it because life wouldn't have any meaning for them if they didn't. That's why I draw cartoons. It's my life.[27]

Like Popeye, Mickey Mouse, Dick Tracy, and other immortal cartoon characters, Charlie Brown, Snoopy, and other members of the *Peanuts* gang will no doubt outlive their creator. The comic strip, however, will not. Sometimes when a cartoonist retires or dies, the syndicate that distributes his or her work will hire another artist to keep the strip going. For example, when Chic Young, the creator of *Blondie,* died, his son Dean took over the strip. This will not happen with *Peanuts.* In 1979, Charles Schulz's children met with lawyers from the United Feature Syndicate to stipulate that no person other than their father will ever be allowed to draw his strip. When Schulz retires, *Peanuts* will retire with him.

That day has finally arrived. On December 14, 1999, Schulz announced he was retiring the *Peanuts* comic strip. The cartoonist was diagnosed with colon cancer in November 1999, shortly before his seventy-seventh birthday. In a statement released to the news media, Schulz explained his decision to retire. "Although I feel better following my recent surgery, I want to focus on my health and my family without worry of a daily deadline."[28]

The last daily *Peanuts* strip appeared in newspapers nationwide on January 3, 2000. The final Sunday strip ran on February 13.

CHAPTER 3

Chuck Jones

On March 25, 1996, the Academy of Motion Picture Arts and Sciences presented a lifetime achievement award to Chuck Jones for his creation of "classic cartoons and cartoon characters whose animated lives have brought joy to our real ones for more than half a century."[29] Although Jones is largely unknown to the public, his cartoon characters are known to almost everyone. Among the characters Jones created are Road Runner and Wile E. Coyote, Marvin the Martian, Pepe Le Pew, Sam Sheepdog, Marc Antony, and Henery Hawk. He also helped develop the characters of Bugs Bunny and Daffy Duck, who were first created by Charles Thorson and Tex Avery, respectively. In all, Jones has directed more than 250 animated cartoons that have entertained millions of viewers and influenced many other cartoonists, writers, and directors. "Can there be anyone in the entire country who has not seen a Chuck Jones picture? I doubt it,"[30] a journalist once wrote.

Chuck Jones takes a break from working on an animated television program.

Acres of Paper

Charles Martin Jones was born on September 21, 1912, in Spokane, Washington. His father, Charles Adams Jones, was an executive with the Metropolitan Life Insurance Company. His mother, Mabel McQuiddy Jones, was a homemaker. When Chuck Jones was just six months old, his father left the insurance business and moved his family to Southern California.

The Jones family struggled in their new surroundings. Charles wanted to run his own business, but each of his ventures failed. Chuck Jones later wrote that his father's business failures paid an unexpected dividend to him, his brother Richard, and his sisters Margaret and Dorothy:

> Every time Father started a new business, he did three things: 1. He bought a new suit. 2. He bought acres of the finest Hammermill bond stationery, complete with the company's letterhead. 3. He bought hundreds of boxes of pencils, also complete with the company name. . . . EVERY TIME FATHER'S BUSINESS FAILED, HIS CHILDREN INHERITED A FRESH LEGACY OF THE FINEST DRAWING MATERIALS IMAGINABLE. Every other child on the block was lucky once a month to get a measly little shoddy little tablet made of measly and shoddy newsprint . . . we Joneses were rolling in tons of lovely white bond paper.[31]

Jones believes that the abundance of drawing materials is one of the reasons why he and his three siblings all became visual artists. "I believe that all children will learn the joy of drawing if encouraged by ample materials, and a strong love from their parents,"[32] he later wrote.

His family's financial woes benefited Chuck Jones in another way as well. As his father struggled to launch a successful business, he moved his family from one furnished home to another. In addition to furniture, most of these homes were stocked with books. Jones perused the shelves of each new home, seeking out new stories to read. Jones's wide and varied reading gave him a strong foundation for his later work.

Among the books Jones found was Mark Twain's *Roughing It*, which Jones later said he read when he was just seven years old. The book includes a chapter on coyotes. It was these pages, Jones later said, that sparked his lifelong interest in the desert predators and led to the creation of one of his most famous characters, Wile E. Coyote.

A Cat, Not a Coyote

The first animal that Jones drew for humorous effect was not a coyote, however. It was a cat. Jones had just turned seven when a striped pinkish-orange cat came up to his back porch in Newport Beach, California. The stray had a wooden tag hanging by a piece of string around his neck that read *JOHNSON*. Jones soon learned that, although the cat looked like an ordinary cat, he did not act like other cats.

> He sat fat and walked thin like other cats, but the resemblance to other cats stopped there. . . . I watched him tiptoe through the dune grass and yellow oyster daisies to the foot of our back porch, then look appraisingly up at me.[33]

Many of young Jones's earliest cartoons show Johnson doing unusual things. For example, the cat had developed a taste for grapefruit, which he preferred to the bacon or eggs Mabel Jones offered him. Jones's mother sometimes gave Johnson a whole grapefruit—uncut and unpeeled—and the family laughed as the cat struggled to tear into it. While Johnson clawed at the large, yellow fruit, Chuck Jones studied the animal's movements. He also observed his family's reaction to the cat's difficulties. Jones did not know it at the time, but he was learning a valuable lesson that he would later use in cartoon animation, as he commented in his autobiography:

Chuck Jones shows off a drawing for "Curiosity Shop," one of the many projects he undertook as the vice president of children's programming for ABC Television.

It took many frustrating hours of chasing grapefruits fruit-lessly around the house before he recognized the wisdom of trapping it by dribbling this elusive adversary to the nearest corner. There it became possible for him to scratch a small flap of rind and burrow greedily in . . . often end-ing up with three-quarters of the rind cocked over his face like a small space helmet. . . . He would saunter out onto the sand, often with only one eye visible. . . . And so John-son's first lesson to me as a future animator was this: Es-chew the ordinary, disdain the commonplace.[34]

Jones learned another valuable lesson from Johnson's antics: the power of exaggeration. If something out of the ordinary is funny, then something more out of the ordinary is even funnier. In an interview, Jones recalled how the cat on the beach gave him ideas for creating humor:

Well, not only did he have his helmet on, but somewhere along the line he had found parts of a dead sea gull and it had left a few feathers on his shoulders. So he was quite a sight. He strolled down to where these girls were having a picnic. And they took one look at this thing with feathers, and the whole business, so that they screamed, and jumped up and ran into the ocean.[35]

Jones later recalled learning another important lesson when he was young. His father disliked President Warren G. Harding and often criticized the president's speaking style. The president, Charles Jones often complained, spoke too long and used too many words. Charles told his children to write like a news re-porter, telling who, what, when, where, and why and leaving out unnecessary embellishments. This proved to be valuable advice to the son who would soon learn to tell complete stories in minutes rather than hours.

Chuck Jones continued to draw throughout his adolescence. At the age of fifteen, Jones dropped out of high school and enrolled in the Chouinard Art Institute, which later became California In-stitute of the Arts. He studied both drawing and painting, but it was drawing that held his interest. At the institute, Jones learned what he later called the first rule of drawing, to "live by the single line—that single honest delineation of the artist's intent. No shad-ing, no multiple lines, no cross-hatching, no subterfuge. Just that line. . . . That is rule 1 of all great drawing. There is no rule 2."[36]

Young Animator

Jones graduated from art school during the Great Depression, the worst economic downturn in American history. Nearly a third of working adults were unemployed nationwide. During the depression, the prices of goods and services fell, including the price of admission to the movies. Perhaps to escape the doldrums of their lives, millions of Americans continued to go to the movies. As a result, the motion picture industry, centered in Hollywood, continued to thrive. Within a few months, Jones was able to find work in a movie studio run by Ubbe Ert Iwerks, one of Walt Disney's original partners and the cocreator of Mickey Mouse.

Jones was hired as a cel washer in 1931. *Cel* is short for celluloid, which was one of the first forms of plastic ever invented. To make an animated movie, artists drew cartoons on the thin, clear celluloid sheets, or cels. One by one, the cels were photographed by a movie camera. After the cels were photographed, the images could be erased and the cel reused. Thus Jones spent his first days in the film industry not drawing pictures but washing them away.

Washing cels was not Jones's dream job, but he worked hard at it. Eventually he was offered a job as an "in-betweener," an artist who fills in the gaps left by the animator so that the action in one cel flows into the next. At last drawing for the movies, Jones worked side by side with established animators such as Walter Lantz, who created Woody Woodpecker. Jones hoped to become an animator himself, but the struggling company folded before Jones was able to move up.

Out of work, Jones supported himself as a portrait artist, selling his drawings for a dollar each. In 1933, he joined Leon Schlesinger Productions, the animation studio that created "Looney Tunes" and "Merry Melodies." The studio sold these brief animated movies, known as animated shorts, to Warner Brothers Studio, which ran them before and after its feature films. Eventually, Warner Brothers purchased the smaller company. Jones stayed with Warner Brothers for thirty years.

At Warner Brothers, Jones worked with other men in their twenties and thirties, all of whom would later be hailed as geniuses: Friz Freleng, Tex Avery, Bob Clampett, Frank Tashlin, and Charles Thorson. All of the animators drew the same cartoon characters, but each had his own style, as Richard Corliss later wrote for *Time* magazine:

Freleng was the anchor, making crisp vaudeville comedies. Clampett bent his stories and pummeled his characters into manic, surreal, endless inventive farce. . . . Avery's mad movies were about movement—motion exploded into violent emotion.[37]

Jones's special gift was characterization, the ability to create unique personalities. Jones later told Chris Farley of the *Chicago Tribune* that he first learned about the importance of characterization in animation while watching Walt Disney's 1933 cartoon "The Three Little Pigs":

For the first time you had three characters that looked alike, but you could tell them apart by the way they acted. Before that . . . the way you tell characters apart is: if they are cute, then they are good. If they are fat and ugly, they are villainous.[38]

Jones realized that the key to creating distinct personalities— as the word *personality* itself suggests—was to endow each character with human traits. In fact, Jones admitted, his characters were more human than animal, "their anatomy abstracted only

Bugs Bunny cocreator Chuck Jones at a Warner Brothers Studio Store in New York in 1993.

The artist at work in his studio in Corona del Mar, California, in 1989.

in the most general way from their prototypes—rabbits, ducks, cats, canaries, etc." The more human the characters appeared, the more lifelike they seemed, and the more believable their predicaments became. For Jones, this was the foundation of his characters' success. "All drama, all comedy, all artistry stems from the believable," Jones later wrote in his autobiography. "All great cartoon characters are based on human behavior we recognize in ourselves. Characters *always* come first."[39]

Jones's characters are not only different from each other but consistent within themselves. This consistency helps the audience anticipate how each character will react to certain situations—an important ingredient in comedy. For example, when Bugs Bunny is handed a lit stick of dynamite, the viewer knows that he will handle it coolly, indifferently. Daffy Duck, on the other hand, will become hysterical. Wile E. Coyote, the Road Runner, Porky Pig—each Warner Brothers cartoon character would react differently to the same situation. As a result, viewers are able not only to follow the action but to anticipate it. This anticipation creates suspense as the viewer wonders just how the expected action will take place. It also makes it possible to create surprises when things do not unfold exactly as the viewer expects. "Variations on the believable—that is the essence of all humor,"[40] Jones later wrote.

Drawing on what he had learned, Jones directed "The Night Watchman," his first animated short, in 1938. In the field of animation, the director not only decides how each scene will be filmed but works with a writer to create the story. The process of sketching out the entire cartoon takes about five weeks. At the time he directed "The Night Watchman," Jones was just twenty-five years old. Over the next twenty-five years, Jones directed another 250 animated shorts—an average of ten a year.

During his career, Jones introduced many new characters, including Pepe Le Pew, Wile E. Coyote, and the Road Runner. In addition to helping develop Bugs Bunny and Daffy Duck, he worked on Porky Pig, Elmer Fudd, Foghorn Leghorn, Sylvester, and Tweety Bird. Jones says he has no favorite among the characters he has brought to life, but he admits that he has a special understanding of Daffy Duck. "When you're doing Daffy Duck, who's a conniving, self-serving person, you realize that—sure, I'm selfish, too,"[41] Jones once told an interviewer. Jones claims that he first became aware of this basic human trait at a party celebrating his sixth birthday:

> The splendid cake, candles bravely ablaze in salute to my maturity, was ample evidence that I had entered manhood. Having blown out the candles . . . I was handed the knife. . . . At this point Daffy Duck must have had for me his earliest beginnings, because I found to my surprise and pleasure that I had no desire to share my cake with anyone. I courteously returned the knife to my mother. I had no need for it, I explained; I would simplify the whole matter by taking the entire cake for myself. . . . My father thereupon . . . escorted me to my room to contemplate in cakeless solitude the meaning of a new word to me: "selfish." To me then, and to Daffy Duck now, "selfish" means "honest but antisocial"; "unselfish" means "socially acceptable but often dishonest." We all *want* the whole cake, but unlike Daffy . . . the coward in the rest of us keeps the Daffy Duck, the small boy in us, under control.[42]

Award-Winning Director

At the time "The Night Watchman" was released, Europe was embroiled in World War II. By 1941, the United States had entered the war. To help with the war effort, Jones created cartoons for the

U.S. Army from 1943 to 1945. In shorts such as "Spies," "Infantry Blues," "Lecture on Camouflage," and "Going Home," Jones did his part to help build morale and relieve the stress of war. Some of the cels from these patriotic films are on display on the fifth floor of the Pentagon in Washington, D.C.

In 1949, Jones introduced the first Road Runner cartoon. That same year, Jones received an Academy Award for "For Scentimental Reasons," a Warner Brothers short starring Pepe Le Pew. The following year, Jones was again awarded the Best Director of an Animated Short Film for "So Much for So Little."

For the next fifteen years, Jones turned out several more masterpieces, including "One Froggy Evening" in 1955. In this unusual cartoon, the only speaking character is a singing frog that is found by a construction worker. Believing he can make a fortune from the creature's talent, the man quits his job and goes into show business, only to find that the frog will not perform when anyone else is around. For this and other films, Jones received several more Academy Award nominations.

Most Memorable Films

Some of Jones's best work grew out of his love of books. Unlike Walt Disney, Jones did not simply retell famous stories. Rather, he parodied them, replacing the characters in the original work with his own creations for humorous effect. For example, in "Robin Hood Makes Good" (1939), Jones cast Bugs Bunny as Robin Hood. In "The Scarlet Pumpernickel" (1950), which is loosely based on *The Scarlet Pimpernel*, Jones used Daffy Duck as the title character.

Jones parodied not only books but operas as well. In "The Rabbit of Seville" (1950), a send-up of Rossini's famous opera *The Barber of Seville*, Bugs Bunny plays a singing barber and Elmer Fudd plays his hapless client. One of Jones's most popular parodies was "What's Opera, Doc?" (1957). It features Bugs Bunny and Elmer Fudd in their classic roles as hunted rabbit and stubborn "wabbit" hunter, but with a twist. During the course of their chase, they stumble into an opera. The two cartoon characters adapt their chase to the setting, dressing in elaborate costumes and singing along with the musical score. In 1992, "What's Opera, Doc?" became the first animated film to be inducted into the National Film Registry.

Jones stayed at Warner Brothers until the studio shut down its cartoon operation in 1962. By then one of the most famous animators of all time, Jones was hired by Metro-Goldwyn-Mayer (MGM) to serve as the head of animation. At MGM, Jones tried his hand at directing the studio's popular Tom and Jerry cartoons. These cartoons, which featured a long-running battle between a cat and a mouse, were more slapstick and violent than the Looney Tunes and Merry Melodies Jones had worked on before. Jones noticeably softened the action in his Tom and Jerry cartoons. "The crudely violent format of the Tom and Jerry cartoons he was given to direct is at odds with his comic sense and style," observed critic Lloyd Rose. "His Tom and Jerry seem not to belong to the world established by the series; they're too sweetnatured."[43] While at MGM, Jones directed an original animated short entitled "The Dot and the Line," a cartoon that earned him a third Academy Award.

Jones left MGM and tried his hand at different projects. He worked with Jim Henson in the development of the popular *Sesame Street* television program. After that, he was hired by the American Broadcasting Company (ABC) to serve as the vice president of children's programming.

After a year at ABC, Jones longed to return to animation. Instead of creating six-minute animated shorts, however, he

Chuck Jones appears with a costumed Bugs Bunny at a ceremony on the first day of issue of a postal service stamp entitled "What's Up, Doc?" in 1997.

decided to direct half-hour animated specials. In 1967, he teamed up with celebrated children's author Theodor Geisel, also known as Dr. Seuss, to animate "How The Grinch Stole Christmas!" First shown on December 18, 1966, the story of the green-skinned holiday hater was a critical and popular success, earning a Peabody Award for television excellence and taking its place beside "A Charlie Brown Christmas," "Rudolph the Red-Nosed Reindeer," and "Frosty the Snowman" as an animated staple of the holiday season.

Throughout the next decade, Jones animated a number of classic stories, including Geisel's "Dr. Seuss's Horton Hears a Who" (1971), Rudyard Kipling's "The White Seal" (1974),

Bugs Bunny is only one of the many cartoon characters created by Chuck Jones and his associates at Warner Brothers Studio.

"RikkiTikki-Tavi" (1975), and "Mowgli's Brothers" (1976). Jones did not parody these classic tales as he did at Warner Brothers; rather, he faithfully brought them to life.

Back to the Basics

For decades, television networks have broadcast the Looney Tunes and Merry Melodies cartoons on Saturday mornings. Impressed by the ongoing popularity of these programs, Warner Brothers hired Jones in 1977 to create a feature-length movie using new animation and twenty-five classic cartoons. The result was 1979's *Bugs Bunny/Road Runner Movie*. The movie proved popular enough to repeat the formula with *Duck Dodgers and the Return of the 24½ Century* and *Bugs Bunny's Bustin' Out All Over*.

In the 1980s, Jones took a long look back over his life in his autobiography, *Chuck Amuck*, a play on the title of a 1953 Daffy Duck cartoon called "Duck Amuck." The book, which included a foreword by filmmaker Steven Spielberg, received excellent reviews. Jones followed the effort with a second book, *Chuck Reducks*, which was published in 1996, the same year that he received his lifetime achievement award from the Academy of Motion Picture Arts and Sciences. When he heard that he was going to receive the award, Jones acknowledged that his career would not have been possible without the contributions of his fellow animators at Warner Brothers:

> I deeply appreciate receiving it, not only for myself, but for the five directors who were the original unit on the Warner Brothers lot. I'm the only one left, and I will proudly accept the award for all of us.[44]

The Academy Award was only one of several lifetime achievement awards Jones has received. He has received similar honors from the Chicago Film Festival, the Houston Film Festival, and the Los Angeles Critics Association. His drawings have been displayed at hundreds of art galleries as well as the Museum of Modern Art in New York. His work, which has been shown on television continuously for the last fifty years, will no doubt continue to entertain children and adults alike far into the future because, as director Peter Bogdanovich put it, Jones's work "remains, like all good fables and only the best of art, both timeless and universal."[45]

CHAPTER 4

Garry Trudeau

Most comic strips appear on the comics page of the newspaper. That is where readers find *Peanuts, Cathy, Beetle Bailey, Dilbert,* and *Blondie,* just to name a few. Sometimes, however, the editors of a newspaper will place a strip that appeals to a special interest in the section of the paper devoted to that interest. For example, *Tank Mc-Namara,* a sports-related strip, often appears in the sports section of the newspaper. Single-panel cartoons such as *Luv Is, Ziggy,* and *Single Slices* have appeared in lifestyle sections. And single-panel political cartoons appear in the editorial pages. One comic strip, however, Garry Trudeau's *Doonesbury,* seems to defy categorization.

Many editors run *Doonesbury* on the comics page, but others place it in the editorial section because of its political content. At some newspapers, *Doonesbury* started out on the comics page but was later moved to the editorial page. The strip's political satire is so potent that in 1975 Trudeau received the Pulitzer Prize for editorial cartooning. It was the first time a strip had ever won the coveted prize. *Doonesbury* remains the only comic strip to straddle these two worlds.

Obscure Beginnings

Garry B. Trudeau was born in New York City in 1948. An intensely private person, Trudeau has not offered his exact birth date to the public. The only details he has provided about his youth are that he grew up in Saranac Lake, New York, enjoyed drawing, and played hockey at Yale University.

It was at Yale that Trudeau first ventured into the world of cartooning. In 1968, during his junior year, Trudeau offered a comic strip named *Bull Tales* to the editor of the *Yale Record,* a campus magazine. The cartoon was accepted and began to appear in the irregularly published journal. Shortly afterward, Trudeau approached Reed Hundt, the editor of the school paper, the *Yale Daily News,* with samples of *Bull Tales.* Hundt looked over the young artist's work, then simply said, "They're all right. We publish pretty much anything."[46]

Bull Tales debuted in the *Yale Daily News* on September 30, 1968. It focused on life at the fictional Walden College, a thinly disguised caricature of Yale. The main character in *Bull Tales* was Michael Doonesbury, a self-styled ladies' man. The strip drew much of its humor from the difficulties of coming of age—the anxiety of being an adult on the outside while still growing up on the inside. In one early strip, Michael Doonesbury is waiting at the train station, thinking to himself, "As the train arrives at New Haven, Mike 'the Man' Doonesbury eagerly waits [sic] his reason for living, i.e., the girl he met during co-ed week. He's had her down for three weekends since, but he's still nervous. Suddenly she appears; a vision of loveliness! O faith, 'tis joy to gaze on her again." Mike extends his arms to embrace the young woman, but she walks right past him, saying, "Get my bags, willya, Creep?" In the final panel, Mike is shown following after the young woman, carrying her luggage and thinking to himself, "Mother, I need you."[47]

In addition to Mike Doonesbury, Trudeau introduced a cast of characters that included B.D., a politically conservative football player; Boopsie, a cheerleader and B.D.'s girlfriend; Mark Slackmeyer, a campus radical; and Zonker Harris, a resident hippie. Trudeau focused not only on the personal struggles of the students, but also on the absurdities of campus life. For example, one early strip poked fun at the school's method of pairing roommates:

> B.D.: (watching TV in dorm room) Well, here I sit at college awaiting my new roommate. I know he'll be cool, since he's computer selected!! You just fill in a form, send it in, and presto! Ideal roommates.
>
> Mike: (entering dorm room) Hi there! My name's Mike Doonesbury. I hail from Tulsa, Oklahoma, and women adore me. Glad to meet you, Roomie!
>
> B.D.: (thinking to himself) Of course there are a few bugs left in the system.[48]

The humor in *Bull Tales* was not always so gentle. Trudeau acidly lampooned the school administration, the athletic program, and campus rules. One memorable strip about the football team caught the eye of a reporter for the *New York Times:*

> The lively exchange between Brian Dowling and Cal Hill was another in the daily accounts of the Yale football team as portrayed through the pen of Garry Trudeau, a student, in his popular *Peanuts*-style comic strip in the *Yale Daily News*, the student newspaper.[49]

Like other cartoonists who had grown up reading *Peanuts*, Trudeau borrowed certain elements from the work of Charles Schulz. For example, B.D.'s comment at the end of the strip quoted above, "Of course there are a few bugs left in the system," rings with Charlie Brown-ish resignation. But in appearance and content, *Bull Tales* more closely resembled the work of another cartoonist, Jules Feiffer.

Like Feiffer, Trudeau sketched his characters loosely with light, thin lines. He also presented speech the same way Feiffer did, showing who was speaking with a short stroke of the pen rather than a speech balloon. Trudeau's content resembled Feiffer's, too. He often portrayed characters gripped by deep anxiety, or angst, and used sarcasm as a main source of humor.

Trudeau did not just copy Feiffer, however. For one thing, Trudeau gave his characters names and told running stories about them, something Feiffer never did. As a result, Trudeau's characters are more sociable and likable than Feiffer's are. In the foreword to a collection of Trudeau's cartoons, author Nora Ephron described her kinship with Trudeau's character Joanie Caucus:

> I have no idea why she's so funny. I just know she kills me. And I think about her all the time. It's not just that I know women like her and that I'm a little like her myself. . . . It's

also that there is something about what she looks like and the way she behaves—so downtrodden and yet plucky, so saggy and yet upright, so droopy-eyed and yet wide awake, so pessimistic and yet deep-down sure that she's on the right track.[50]

From Bull Tales to Doonesbury

Trudeau graduated from Yale in 1970 and enrolled in the Yale School of Art to pursue a master of fine arts degree. Shortly thereafter, Trudeau heard from Jim Andrews and John McMeel, the cofounders of Universal Press Syndicate. Andrews and McMeel wanted the comic strip, and Trudeau liked the idea of taking the strip to a national audience. The newspaper executives, however, feared that some readers might be offended by the name of the strip, which is a slang term for untrue or exaggerated stories. At their urging, Trudeau renamed the strip *Doonesbury*. On October 26, 1970, Universal Press Syndicate launched the strip in twenty-eight newspapers.

When *Doonesbury* first appeared, Trudeau was just twenty-two years old. Already a gifted humorist, Trudeau still had much to learn about creating a daily comic strip. Fortunately Trudeau's editor, Jim Andrews, was willing to invest time and attention in the young man he termed "a comic genius." Recalling this period, Trudeau later said:

Doonesbury *creator Garry Trudeau has been described as a "comic genius."*

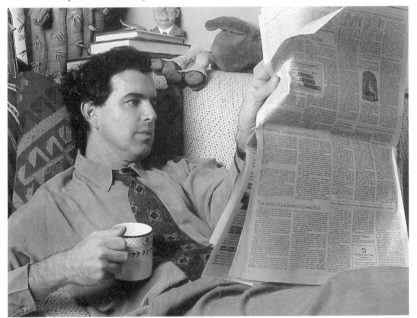

If you have a good editor, as I had for ten years in Jim Andrews, you come to realize that the inner life of a comic strip is a very fragile ecosystem. It has its own rules, its own time frames, its own internal logic. That logic may be completely askew, but if you tinker with it the chances are pretty good the whole thing will collapse.[51]

Controversy and More Controversy

As he moved his characters from Walden College to Walden Commune, Trudeau widened the scope of his comic strip, commenting on issues such as the Vietnam War, draft dodging, racism, and feminism. Trudeau's political commentary did not seem funny to some editors, and several quickly dropped the strip. Other editors carried *Doonesbury* until Trudeau crossed what they believed to be the bounds of good taste. For some editors, this occurred in May 1972, when Trudeau's character Zonker Harris blamed Attorney General John Mitchell for the shooting deaths of Vietnam War protesters at Kent State University.

Another firestorm erupted when Zonker mentioned his love of marijuana to one of his day-care charges. Thousands of parents, teachers, and school administrators phoned and wrote their local newspapers complaining about the bad example set by the strip. Afterward, Charles Kilpatrick, an editor for the *San Antonio News*, wrote to United Press Syndicate president John McMeel about the uproar:

> I also had threats from Abilene and Paris, Texas. . . . Paris even ran a letter of apology to their readers and said they would refuse to deliver the entire section if it happened again. I think the thing that disturbed most of the publishers is that professional school administrators were the leaders of the protests.[52]

Trudeau never apologized for the content of his strips. Indeed, in a speech before a convention of newspaper editors in 1971, he was defiant:

> I am frequently compelled to answer the question of whether or not this strip is a fair commentary on the present social scene. It does, however, seem to me that what is lacking in such a question is a fundamental understanding of the nature of comedy. The derivatives of humor on comic strips have always been based on hyperbole, exaggeration and overstatement. Satire has always been formulated through the

expansion and refraction of the truth. Cartoonists *do* concern themselves with the truth, but if they delivered it straight, they would totally fail in their roles as humorists. Therefore, I feel no obligation to be "fair" in any absolute sense to a subject simply because certain individuals are sensitive to it.[53]

Watergate

The outrage Trudeau provoked by his commentary on the Vietnam War, Kent State, and drug usage was great, but the biggest flap over his work was still ahead. In 1972, five men were arrested for breaking into the Democratic National Headquarters in the Watergate Hotel in Washington. For months, Republican president Richard Nixon and other White House officials denied any prior knowledge of the break-in or of any conspiracy to cover up the scandal. News reporters at the *Washington Post* continued to pursue the story, however, slowly revealing evidence of White House involvement. Finally, the Senate looked into the scandal. One by one, White House officials denied involvement in the operation. Through it all, Trudeau mocked the White House's claims of innocence.

Whereas news reporters had to be careful about their accusations in order to protect their own credibility, Trudeau felt free to say what critics of the White House really believed: that Nixon, Mitchell, and other officials were deeply involved in the scandal. Trudeau drew pictures of the White House and above it wrote what he thought was being said behind closed doors.

Once again, Trudeau focused on former attorney general John Mitchell, who strongly professed his innocence. While Mitchell awaited trial on charges stemming from the break-in, Trudeau savaged the former attorney general. One strip showed Mark Slackmeyer, who worked at a radio station, reading a news report about Mitchell:

Good news, kiddies! Time for another exclusive WBBY "Watergate Profile"! Today's obituary—John Mitchell! John Mitchell, the former U.S. Attorney General has in recent weeks been repeatedly linked with both the Watergate caper and its cover-up. It would be a disservice to Mr. Mitchell and his character to prejudge the man, but everything known to date could lead one to conclude he's guilty. That's guilty! Guilty, guilty, guilty, guilty![54]

The humor of this strip arose from the tension between Slackmeyer's duty to presume Mitchell innocent and his overpowering urge to pronounce him guilty. In this one strip, Trudeau managed to lampoon Mitchell, who maintained his innocence despite all evidence to the contrary, as well as members of the press, who self-righteously had passed judgment on the former attorney general.

Trudeau's critique of the press went largely unnoticed, but his mockery of Mitchell caused an uproar. For many supporters of the White House, Trudeau's attack on Mitchell symbolized a liberal press gone berserk, and thousands of readers complained to their editors or canceled their subscriptions. Even newspapers that had stuck by Trudeau in the past, such as the *Los Angeles Times* and the *Boston Globe*, chose to not run the "Guilty!" episode, believing it was unfair to pronounce a verdict on a pending trial. Many other newspapers dropped the strip altogether.

Unmoved by the criticism, Trudeau continued to poke fun at the legal maneuvering of White House officials. Once members of Nixon's staff resigned, attention turned toward the president himself. In 1974, Congress began to consider removing the president from office, an action known as impeachment. When the president's lawyer, Robert St. Clair, argued that such action was unwarranted, Trudeau showed two members of Congress reacting to the statement:

Congressman #1: No impeachable offense! How can St. Clair keep babbling that?

Congressman #2: Especially since the President left no part of the Constitution unviolated.

#1: Obstruction of justice, hush money payments, secret bombings, 25 top aides convicted or indicted...

#2: My Lord, what does it take?! WHAT DOES IT TAKE?! (both sigh)

#1: If only he'd knock over a bank or something...

#2: By George, we'd have him then![55]

In another cartoon, Trudeau showed Nixon speechwriter Pat Buchanan thinking of how to phrase a resignation speech for the president. This partisan cartoon caused the Providence *Bulletin* to move the cartoon from the comic pages to the editorial pages. The action made sense to Allan Parachini, who wrote in the *Columbia Journalism Review*, "Considering the consistent reader outrage at

Poking fun at political figures is a specialty of Garry Trudeau.

periodic censorship, more papers may find that solution the palatable one."[56] Parachini was right. Many other newspapers followed the *Bulletin*'s lead, transferring *Doonesbury* to the editorial section.

Eventually secret White House tape recordings proved that Trudeau's musings about goings-on inside the White House had not been too far from the truth. Once the tapes became public, Congress prepared to impeach the president. Knowing that he did not have enough votes to survive impeachment, Nixon resigned. John Mitchell was tried and found guilty, as were other members of Nixon's staff. These events vindicated Trudeau and silenced many of his critics. In 1975 Trudeau received a Pulitzer Prize for his editorial cartooning work of the previous year.

Even Trudeau's Pulitzer Prize proved controversial. It was the first time that a non-editorial-page cartoon had ever received the prize for editorial cartooning. It was also the first time that a comic strip artist had received the award. Many traditional editorial cartoonists were upset that a comic strip had been selected over their single-panel cartoons. They believed it was an unfair comparison. The Editorial Cartoonists' Society passed a resolution to condemn the Pulitzer Prize committee. Assured that his award could not be revoked, Trudeau himself expressed support for the resolution.

Not everyone was taken with Trudeau's work. Charles Schulz, the creator of *Peanuts*, found *Doonesbury* too remote from everyday life to be of much value. "I deal in more social issues in one month than *Doonesbury* deals in all year," Schulz once said. "I deal with issues that are much more important than drawing four pictures of the White House."[57]

Taking Comics a Step Further

For critic Robert C. Harvey, it was the four pictures of the White House that were the problem:

> Visually, the Doonesbury of this period was about as dull as it is possible for a comic strip to be. . . . Panel after panel, the pictures stay the same while the political commentary drones on.[58]

Harvey had to admit, however, that Trudeau's static drawing style "adds a layer of meaning to the strip." He points out that when the picture does not change for the first three panels, any change in the fourth panel—however small—"draws attention to itself. . . . Thus a single fourth-panel variation on an otherwise repetitive series of panels becomes a powerful device for Trudeau's editorializing."[59]

Harvey points out that even when the fourth panel does not change, Trudeau is making a statement. For example, in one strip Michael Doonesbury is watching a news report on television. In all four panels, nothing changes, not even the expression on Michael's face. The words coming out of the television have no impact at all on Michael. According to Harvey, that is Trudeau's point. "It is as if the strip is presenting us with two worldviews," Harvey noted. "The world we seem to create out of custom . . . has no bearing upon or relationship to the real world of concrete details."[60]

Trudeau's static, "photocopied" strips were unlike any comics that had come before. Because Trudeau did not blend the words and the action as other cartoonists did, *Doonesbury* looked different than other strips, and this forced people to think about the strip differently. "Trudeau has taken the art of the comic strip a step further," Harvey observed. "He has made the very nature of the medium—the relationship of word and picture—the vehicle of his humor and his comment."[61]

Trudeau has become known for another visual innovation: drawing a symbol to represent a person rather than drawing the person's likeness. Rather than draw a picture of President George Bush, for example, Trudeau drew a circle of tiny lines that represented empty speech. For Bush's vice president, Dan Quayle, Trudeau drew a floating feather, suggesting that he was a political and intellectual lightweight. Trudeau portrayed President Bill Clinton with a waffle, representing the president's tendency to change his mind, or waffle, on issues.

Social Issues

Politicians have remained one of Trudeau's targets through the years, but he has also used his characters to comment on a wide range of social issues. For example, Joanie Caucus entered the strip in the 1970s as a feminist who took a job at the Walden Day Care Center. As the years progressed, Joanie went to law school, married, and had a son. She was later concerned about dropping her son off with a baby-sitter so that she could keep working. One strip with Joanie's young son, Jeffrey, demonstrated society's hot debate regarding placing children in day care as opposed to parenting young children at home. Joanie's character empathized with many working women in America when she faced the parenting dilemma while talking with baby-sitter Mrs. Wicker:

Joanie: Sorry we're late again, Mrs. Wicker.

Wicker: No skin off my nose. Of course the other kids have started.

Joanie: Started what?

Wicker: Watching the tube. You got this week's check?

Joanie: (rummaging in purse) Uh . . . yes. You let the children watch much television?

Wicker: What'd you expect? Violin lessons? C'mon, kid.

Joanie: We're looking for someone better than you, you know.

Wicker: Good luck.[62]

Trudeau also tackled health issues. He invented Mr. Butts, an anthropomorphic cigarette who worked for the tobacco industry by recruiting new smokers. Mr. Butts tormented Mike Doonesbury's imagination while Mike worked for an advertising agency. The talking cigarette tried to convince Mike that smoking was not harmful. The sarcasm helped Trudeau show readers his disdain for the tobacco industry's efforts to convince young people to smoke.

Trudeau returned to the theme of drug use in the fall of 1996, drawing six strips that took issue with outlawing the medicinal use of marijuana. Until that time, some states allowed doctors to prescribe the drug to relieve intense discomfort in terminal patients who were dying of painful diseases such as cancer. The specific controversy concerned California attorney general Dan Lungren's decision to shut down the Cannabis Buyer's Club that sold marijuana for medicinal purposes. Trudeau mocked Lungren's policy, and according to one report, the California attorney general was outraged:

Lungren said the comic strip is corrupting our youth and should be "canceled" or should run with a disclaimer. He said

the cartoon uses "misinformation in an attempt to lend credibility to the Cannabis Buyer's Club."[63]

In 1997, Trudeau aimed his satire at Nike, a company which makes sports shoes, garments, and equipment. When news reports claimed that the sporting goods giant operated factories in Vietnam under unsafe and inhumane working conditions, *Doonesbury* took Nike to task. In a series of cartoons that began in May 1997, Trudeau sent one of his strip's characters, Kim, the last orphan airlifted out of Saigon, back to Vietnam to check out the Nike factory. Kim had

Garry Trudeau appears at a book signing.

learned that she might have a cousin working there and wanted to make sure the reports about Nike were false. The series lasted throughout June and detailed many infractions of employee rights, alerting Americans to the fact that all was not well with corporate industry in foreign countries.

Trudeau has never relaxed his attacks on individuals or organizations that he believes are too powerful, pompous, unfeeling, uncaring, or greedy. In doing so, he has encouraged millions of Americans to take a second look at controversial issues. As one reporter suggests, Trudeau's brand of satire is not only humorous but insightful and long-lasting:

> Garry Trudeau has shown that great satire needn't be instantly disposable. For almost 30 years, *Doonesbury* has provided a hilarious perspective on modern America, combining insightful political commentary with inspired silliness. . . . Trudeau wasn't afraid to court controversy or to stretch limits of what people expected to see on the funny pages. Indeed, his creation now often appears on editorial rather than humor pages. . . . Garry Trudeau continues to make a major contribution to American culture.[64]

CHAPTER 5

Cathy Guisewite

In April 1976, executives at Universal Press Syndicate opened a package containing eighteen cartoons and a letter from Cathy Guisewite, a Michigan advertising executive. Dated April 12, 1976, the letter read:

> Dear Mr. Andrews,
>
> Chances are, the world isn't screaming for a new comic strip as loudly as I'm hoping. But I have an idea for a new strip that the world might like a lot if someone besides my mother ever got a chance to see it.
>
> So here it is.
>
> It's a strip about being single in a pretty unusual time. About being a woman in a pretty unusual time. . . . *Cathy* is a young lady who wants very much to make it on her own. Her convictions just aren't always as strong as her emotions.[65]

Although crudely drawn, the strip appealed to the Universal Press Syndicate executives. "We felt that Cathy the character was real," remembered Lee Salem, the managing editor. "That's what struck us about her work. It deals with what it's like to be young, single, and working today." Within an hour and a half of opening the package, the executives all agreed to offer Guisewite a contract. "Given the sentiments of the day, we thought there would be room for a strip that deals with young women,"[66] said Lee Salem.

Salem and the other executives were right. *Cathy* debuted on November 22, 1976, in sixty newspapers. By 1999, that number had grown to more than fourteen hundred. Every day, millions of readers turn to the funny page to check up on Cathy's dating woes, her relationship with her parents, her shopping disasters, and her stressful work life.

A Mother's Encouragement

Cathy Guisewite was born on September 5, 1950, in Dayton, Ohio, but spent much of her childhood and teenage years in the small town of Midland, Michigan. Her father, Bill, was a president of an advertising agency, and her mother, Anne, worked as an advertising copywriter. Guisewite also has two sisters, Mary Anne and Michelle, whom she calls Mickey.

At the age of six, Guisewite wrote her first story. Her mother sent it off to a magazine to see if it could be published. Guisewite later joked about her mother's excessive pride in her children's work. "Most mothers tape their children's work to the refrigerator door. Mine would send them off to the Museum of Modern Art."[67]

The story was rejected, but Anne Guisewite's dreams of success for her daughters did not fade. She made a point of exposing Cathy, Mary Anne, and Michelle to the arts. "She took us to museums and foreign films, and I hated everything she dragged us to," Cathy later recalled. "I resented my mom for not being the kind of mother who sat home baking all day."[68]

Anne also encouraged her children to make their own greeting cards and illustrated books. When Cathy Guisewite was in college, she created such a book, "A College Girl's Mother's Guide to Survival," as a gift for her mother on Mother's Day. Further convinced of her daughter's talent, Anne sent the book to Tom Wilson, a vice president at the American Greetings Corporation. Wilson expressed encouragement but returned the book without publishing it.

Cathy Guisewite drew cartoons about herself as a way of showing her family what was going on in her life.

While pursuing an English degree at the University of Michigan, Guisewite continued to send her mother cartoons about college life. In 1972, she graduated with a bachelor of arts degree.

Following in her parents' footsteps, she took a job as a copywriter at the Campbell-Ewald advertising agency in Detroit. A year later, she moved to the Norman Prady agency and began writing newspaper and magazine ads as well as radio commercials. In 1974, she joined W. B. Donner and Company, a large advertising agency located in Southfield, Michigan. Guisewite began to make a name for herself as a radio-commercial writer. "She could sit down and turn out ten scripts in a day, and they'd all be good," one of her colleagues later said. Guisewite found the work stimulating. "Creativity was encouraged even on mediocre accounts," Guisewite remembered. "It's where I trained my brain to write with a sense of humor."[69]

In 1976, Guisewite became the first female vice president in Donner's history. Her devotion to her job caused problems in her personal life, however. "As I became more involved with my work, my love life began to fall apart," Guisewite recalled in one interview. "I would try to meet men and nothing would happen, or I'd meet men I just didn't want to go out with at all. As a result, I started spending a lot of evenings at home writing about my feelings in a diary—something my mother had encouraged me to do when I was younger."[70]

Sometimes Guisewite illustrated her diary entries with simple drawings. "I used to eat everything in the kitchen every night . . . and sort of wait for Mr. Wrong to call," she later recalled. "So the first comic strip I drew was a picture of what I looked like sitting there waiting and writing and eating."[71] Guisewite found that the process of cartooning helped her feel better: "When I saw myself in drawing, I began to see humor in situations that wouldn't otherwise have seemed funny."[72]

Submission and Syndication

To keep her parents updated on her life, Guisewite began to send them cartoons instead of letters. Once again, Anne Guisewite believed that her daughter's work was ripe for publication. She began to research the market for the comic strip, even taking it upon herself to contact Tom Wilson, the creator of the comic Ziggy, for advice about breaking into the field.

Anne drew up a list of syndicates to contact and mailed it to her daughter. Worried that her mother would submit her drawings for her, Guisewite assembled the package that she sent to Universal Press Syndicate. In her biographical note in the International Museum of Cartoonists, Guisewite described the incident as being "forced by mother to send humiliating drawings of my miserable love life to Universal Press Syndicate in 1976."[73]

Not only was Cathy one of the first comic strips about a working woman to be created by a woman, it was also one of the most autobiographical. Similarities between the real Cathy and the cartoon Cathy include their long dark hair and wide-eyed expressions. They both are working women, both are devoted daughters, and both hate wearing swimsuits. At first, Guisewite worried about naming the strip after herself. "Not only did the character resemble me a little physically, but what I was writing about was quite personal," she later said. "I didn't want friends calling me up the next day, saying, 'Idiot, why did you say that about yourself?'" Guisewite bought a baby-naming book to see if she could find a good alternative, but no other name quite worked. "She *had* to be 'Cathy.' To be, well, *me*," Guisewite concluded. "She's so close to how I think. Using the same name can be a little embarrassing at times, but it helps me keep her true to life."[74]

Charles Schulz, the creator of *Peanuts*, has gotten to know Guisewite professionally and personally. While he sees the similarities between the creator of *Cathy* and its main character, Schulz says they are definitely two different people, both of whom have a lot to offer the world:

> The Cathy in Cathy Guisewite's strip is really not the Cathy Guisewite I know. I can tell them apart with no trouble at all. The comic strip *Cathy* points out for us just how much trouble life is for a young working girl. She shrieks in agony, laughs with delight, and works very hard. I don't know if Cathy Guisewite ever shrieks in agony, but I know she laughs easily, and works very hard. . . . It is very, very difficult to make [a comic strip] better and better, and this is what Cathy Guisewite has been doing. *Cathy* gets better every day.[75]

One improvement Guisewite has made in the strip has been in the area of drawing. In *The Art of the Funnies*, Robert C. Harvey

referred to *Cathy* as a "poorly drawn" comic strip, "flat and gray as a TV test pattern in black and white," that "veers toward technical incompetence."[76] Guisewite has joked about her lack of drawing ability, admitting that her syndicate has helped her with "little things—like connecting the heads to the bodies."[77] She has studied other strips to learn how to improve her art. From *Beetle Bailey*, she learned how to render visual motion such as a flurry of activity. From *Peanuts*, she learned to create better facial expressions. The progress has been steady, as one critic observed:

> As Miss Guisewite's artistry has developed over the years, Cathy has changed in appearance. She was originally somewhat weakly defined, with shaky lines and sparse strands of hair, and she always wore pants and a long-sleeved shirt with a heart in the middle. Today, she still has no nose and no profile, but she is better defined, and she wears an assortment of outfits.[78]

Even Harvey admits that Guisewite has developed a drawing style that works. "Even in [*Cathy*] . . . the visuals are a powerful component of the form: it is difficult to imagine [it] drawn in any other way."

Most fans of *Cathy* turn to the comic not for its artwork, but because they admire Guisewite's courage to "tell it like it is" about being a single woman. To do this, Guisewite makes fun of both her own and her cartoon character's weaknesses. Guisewite believes that such honesty is the thing that has made the strip so successful.

> I think the strip's continuing popularity is because it shows the weaker moment we all have. It's hard to admit you came in from a date and ate an entire cheesecake. At a time when most women appear to have it under control, it's a relief to see a woman who doesn't have it under control and deals with problems in her own way.[80]

One of Cathy's chief frailties is her inability to express her feelings directly or positively. Using "thought balloons," Guisewite allows the reader to know what Cathy is feeling. Instead of having Cathy express those feelings in a way that might make the situation better, Guisewite has Cathy stew about them for several panels, then release the pent-up emotion in an indirect way, such as overeating, tearing up clothing, or shrieking. The gap between what Cathy feels and what she does is so great that it strikes the reader as funny.

The humor in *Cathy* is similar to the humor in *Peanuts*, though the effects are achieved in exactly opposite ways. In

Cathy Guisewite poses with a soft sculpture of her popular Cathy character.

Peanuts, the characters are children, but they respond to stress as adults; Cathy is an adult, but she responds to stress as a child. When Charlie Brown is frustrated, he becomes philosophical; when Cathy is frustrated, she acts out. In both cases, the non sequitur response is so far out of the norm that it is funny. In addition, Cathy's immature reactions endear her to adults who often wish they could act like children again. When Cathy runs screaming from a business meeting, tears up work instead of doing it, or shouts at salespeople, she acts out the adult fantasy of returning to childhood.

In fairness to the cartoon Cathy, her parents have not done much to encourage her to grow up. Her mother, especially, continues to treat her as a child. Cathy tries to assert her independence but often ends up proving she is still a child. Guisewite described one such strip:

> One of my best strips . . . is one where Cathy says, "I love you Mom, but I'll never be like you. I'll never think like you, I'll never act like you, I'll never look like you." And Mom says, "Oh, I know, I used to say the exact same thing to my mom, and I wound up thinking just like her, acting just like her, looking like her. See, you're just like me already." And Cathy runs from the room screaming, and Mom says, "Oh, isn't that cute, that's just what I used to do."[81]

The conflict between mother and daughter is one of the most popular themes in the strip. Even though the relationship between the cartoon Cathy and her mother is wrapped in real love, it is also wrapped in conflict. Cathy's mother wants her daughter to succeed in business, but not be so successful that she never makes time to visit with her. She wants her daughter to clean out her closets, but doesn't want Cathy to give away those clothes that are not worn out yet. The episodes show how hard it is for children to become independent of their parents and for parents to give independence to their children. In one strip written in the '80s, Cathy's father asks his wife if she was able to grant Cathy her independence during a lunch outing:

Dad: How was your mother-daughter lunch with Cathy?

Mom: I had the time of my life!

Dad: You didn't butt into things that were none of your business?

Mom: Oh, yes! I butted.

Dad: She didn't snap at you?

Mom: Oh, yes! She snapped!

Dad: You fought?

Mom: (smiling) We fought. We attacked. We made each other totally berserk . . . and then we plopped down together and split a cheesecake!!

Dad: (thinking) Understanding one woman is tough. Understanding two of them is beyond comprehension.[82]

"I think the truest thing in the comic strip is Cathy's relationship with her mom," Guisewite once said. "It's a rich tangle of genuine devotion, anxiety, frustration, friendship, love, a need for dependence and a need for independence. Lots of butting heads. Around Mom, I still behave like a six-year-old. Stubborn. Obstinate. Belligerent. Taking offense where none was intended. Being contrary for the joy of being contrary."[83]

Fashion and Health

Considering that fashion and health are often hot topics for single women, it is only natural for Guisewite to throw her character into some frustrating situations involving both of these interests. One of the recurring characters in *Cathy* is a nameless department store salesclerk who usually has a pencil tucked behind her ear. Guisewite says this woman always waits on Cathy whether the character is buying shoes or chocolate or ordering dinner at a fancy restaurant. She admits she wanted the woman to be a symbol of conflict for Cathy, but there is another reason, too:

> The Sales Clerk, who was the same woman in every store and institution Cathy went in, was a symbol of all clashes with bureaucracy. She was also always the same woman because that's the only way I could draw a sales clerk.[84]

No matter what Cathy is searching for, each shopping trip usually breaks down into a mental and emotional tug-of-war with the nameless saleswoman. One strip involved the saleswoman's use of a new technique to confuse Cathy and snag a sale—guilt:

Cathy: (Holding dress from rack) This is nice.

Saleswoman: It's 100% linen. You'll have to iron it every 15 seconds.

Cathy: The color is great.

Saleswoman: Light peach. It'll get filthy. You'll spend a fortune at the cleaners.

Cathy: I really like it.

Saleswoman: It's too casual for the office, too tailored for a date. You'd be throwing perfectly good money down the drain!!

Cathy: Perfect! Ring it up! I'll take it!!

Saleswoman: (thinking) Nothing moves them into action like the sound of their mother's voice.[85]

Cathy's continuous fight with fashion has focused on swimwear in countless strips, always leaving Cathy feeling completely dissatisfied with her body. The theme became such a pattern each new swimwear season that in 1995 Dupont Lycra® published a "Cathy Swimwear Survival Calendar" to help advertise its spandex fiber.

When Guisewite started creating *Cathy*, she was single, as was her main character. The unmarried status of the main character was one of the biggest reasons the syndicate bought the strip. In 1998, Guisewite married Chris Wilkinson, a forty-seven-year-old screenwriter. Although the strip mirrors her life in many ways, Guisewite plans to keep Cathy single and in disarray. "I'm determined not to let my own great relationship ruin the comic," Guisewite said when she announced her engagement. "I was single a long time, so I don't have to be single to write about it."[86]

Guisewite's comic brilliance has earned her many awards. She received an Emmy in 1987 for the animated special *Cathy*. In 1992 the National Cartoonist Society honored her with a Reuben Award as the Outstanding Cartoonist of the Year. In 1997 Guisewite published a cookbook titled *Girl Food,* which boasts a recipe for "After Five Hundred and Two Dinners and Four Hundred and Twenty-Seven Cups of Coffee, I Think It's Time to Get Serious Marry Me Mousse."

After twenty-five years of focusing on one central character in her strip, Guisewite is often asked if she has trouble coming up with fresh ideas for *Cathy*. She answers that she has plenty of material right at hand:

> In the '70s, I thought I'd be a success as a woman if I
> earned my own way. In the '80s, I thought I'd be a success
> as a woman if I were the president of a billion dollar com-

pany, had a sensitive soul-mate husband, two bilingual children, buns of steel, and a compost heap. In the '90s, I pretty much feel I'm a success if I can get through the afternoon without eating a cheesecake. . . . For all the people who wonder where I get my ideas, how much do I really need to make up?[87]

CHAPTER 6

Matt Groening

Matt Groening has done what no other cartoonist has been able to accomplish in the history of cartooning. His hit television program *The Simpsons* has become the longest-running prime-time animated series in history, outlasting such cartoon classics as *The Flintstones* and *The Jetsons*. Already in syndication, early episodes of *The Simpsons* are replayed at least once a day in most American cities. Bart, Lisa, Maggie, Homer, and Marge are such well-known characters that people often refer to them by first name only. Catchphrases from the program such as "Don't have a cow," "Eat my shorts," "Kowabunga," and "D'oh!" have shaped the speech of millions.

From Portland to Los Angeles

Matt Groening entered the world on February 15, 1954, in Portland, Oregon. His parents, Homer and Margaret, his sisters, Maggie and Lisa, and his brother, Mark, lived in Portland for several years. Homer Groening was a cartoonist and a filmmaker, and he owned an advertising agency. The young Matt Groening thought his father was "the hippest dad in the neighborhood," and he admired his success in his chosen profession. "My dad is a cartoonist, film maker, and writer who has lived by his wits," Groening once said. "By example, he showed that you could do whatever you wanted in life—that a certificate didn't matter and that you could do creative stuff."[88]

Besides serving as a role model for his son, Homer furnished Matt with many examples of creative work. As an advertising professional, Homer received many industry magazines for free. Matt spent countless hours browsing through his father's magazines, looking at the work of other artists and studying their styles.

The young Groening was a fan of the comics, especially Walt Kelly's *Pogo*, Charles Schulz's *Peanuts*, and *Mad* magazine. He also enjoyed the illustrated works of Dr. Seuss. Groening soon began to emulate his heroes by doing drawings of his own. He later explained that when he was in school, he drew all the time, even when he was not supposed to:

I was unable to sit there quietly while the teacher was droning on and on, and I passed the time by squirming and drawing. When the teacher confiscated my cartoons, I was incapable of still keeping still so I drew on the desk. And then I would get caught for drawing on the desk and the teacher would draw this circle in chalk on the black-board and make me stick my nose in it. . . . I was an extreme case . . . my big mouth got me in trouble quite a bit.[89]

Although Groening admits that he was not the most well behaved student, he adds that some of his teachers were not only unfair, but downright mean. Groening started keeping a diary to record some of their treatment. Today he uses the comments in his diary as story and character ideas for *The Simpsons*, especially the episodes involving Bart Simpson.

Matt Groening, creator of The Simpsons, *poses with a live duck.*

Groening drew his first comic strip when he was a young boy in Portland. The strip was inspired, in part, by Groening's adventures in an abandoned zoo located near his home. Groening and his friends hid in caves that grizzly bears had lived in and played war games on the woody hillsides. With that kind of an environment to explore every day, it is easy to understand why his first strip involved animals and trees. Groening called his roughly drawn comic *Tales of the Enchanted Forest*.

Groening continued to draw the comic after his family moved to Los Angeles right before he entered high school. Groening thought his comic was funny, but his friends often failed to "get" his gags. The problem, he later explained, was that he simply did not draw very well:

> I used to draw all sorts of animals back in high school . . . but my bears didn't really look like bears, they looked sort of like big mice, and my mice looked like dogs, and people couldn't really tell what the dogs were. . . . Well, I had one rabbit character and they said, "Ah! A rabbit!" So that's why I stuck with rabbits.[90]

Groening was in high school during a time of great cultural change in the United States, especially in California. Students were protesting the war in Vietnam, rebelling against school dress codes with long hair and short skirts, and generally questioning authority. Groening was swept up in the subversive mood, mocking the institution of student government by mounting a humorous campaign for student body president. As the head of a group called Students for Decency, Groening ran with the slogan, "If you're against decency, what are you for?"[91] Once elected, Groening attempted to rewrite the student government constitution to give himself absolute power. He failed to change the constitution, but did not fail to get a laugh.

While in high school, Groening applied to two colleges: Harvard University and Evergreen State College. His application to Harvard was rejected, so he traveled to Olympia, Washington, to attend Evergreen State. While there he studied literature and journalism and worked on the college newspaper, the *Copper Point Journal*. One of the members of the newspaper staff was a student named Lynda Barry. Like Groening, Barry drew cartoons, but her work was unlike anything Groening had known before. "She was this crazy girl who did the wildest cartoons I'd ever seen and was very inspiring to me," Groening later told a reporter. "She showed me you could do cartoons about anything."[92]

Despite their shared interest in cartoons, neither Groening nor Barry imagined they would one day earn money from their creative pastime. "My goal in life was to be a writer, and hers was to be a fine artist," Groening said in a 1989 interview. "We did cartooning as this other thing and neither of us expected it to be part of how we paid the rent."[93]

Life in Hell

After graduating from college in 1977, Groening moved to Los Angeles with dreams of becoming a writer. He arrived in the city on a sweltering August day, and his car immediately broke down. He rented an apartment in "a neighborhood full of drug peddling, random fights, [and] police helicopters"[94] and took a series of dead-end jobs to support himself. Instead of writing letters to his friends about his experiences in Los Angeles, Groening sent them cartoons entitled, simply, *Life in Hell*.

Over the years, Groening's comic sense had sharpened, but his drawing skills remained crude. Not surprisingly, *Life in Hell* featured

Matt Groening holds up two books that feature cartoon characters he created.

a family of rabbits—Binky and Sheba and their son, Bongo. Groening also managed to draw two short humans named Akbar and Jeff. "I had no idea I was going to make cartooning a career," Groening later recalled. "I was doing it merely to assuage my profound sense of self-pity at being stuck in this scummy little apartment in Hollywood."[95]

Before long, *Life in Hell* started to help Groening pay the rent. He collected the cartoons into homemade comic books, to sell at the record store where he worked. He sold the photocopied books for $2 each. At first sales were slow, but by the sixth edition Groening was printing five-hundred copies of *Life in Hell*.

Groening also began to submit his work to professional publications. Like most artists and cartoonists, Groening experienced quite a few rejections. Despite his lack of success, however, Groening did not give up. He continued to send out his drawings despite their obvious shortcomings. His persistence paid off, as he later explained:

> I knew my stuff didn't look too hot, but I kept it up, no matter how crummy the drawing was. My more talented friends grew up, got mature and put aside cartooning for more serious pursuits. They're now boring old doctors and lawyers and business execs. I, on the other hand, went on to hit the doodler's jackpot.[96]

In 1977, the punk magazine *Wet* published the first installment of *Life in Hell*. In 1979, Groening began to write articles for the *L.A. Reader*, an alternative weekly newspaper, and one year later it too began to carry *Life in Hell*. The cartoon did not really catch on until the following year, when Groening made an important discovery about his work. Up until then, his main character, Binky, was "really hostile, ranting and raving," often challenging the readers directly. Starting in 1981, Groening began to "make the rabbit a victim instead of an aggressor." Readers stopped fearing the rabbit and began to sympathize with him. "The second I made the rabbit a victim, people started liking the strip. The more tragedies that befell this poor little rodent, the more positive response I got,"[97] Groening later recalled.

By 1983, some twenty newspapers—mostly alternative weeklies—carried *Life in Hell*. Slowly the cartoon began to work its way out of the newspapers and onto the bulletin boards, refrigerators, and office doors of its loyal readers. Critics began to notice the hard-edged comic as well. Richard Harrington of the *Washington*

Post praised the strip as "funny and fatalistic, rude and revealing, touching raw nerves, funny bones, and heartstrings all at the same time."[98]

One of the biggest fans of the strip worked at the *L.A. Reader* with Groening. Her name was Deborah Caplan. A member of the paper's advertising department, Caplan believed *Life in Hell* could be even more popular than it was. In 1984, she published a collection of Groening's cartoons with the title *Love Is Hell*. The initial printing of two-thousand copies sold out immediately, so she printed twenty thousand more.

Despite his limited drawing skills, Matt Groening persisted as a cartoonist until he "hit the doodler's jackpot."

In 1985, Caplan and Groening left the *L.A. Reader* to start Life in Hell, Inc. Over the next three years, the two published three more books: *Work Is Hell*, *School Is Hell*, and *Childhood Is Hell*. They also got married. Speaking of his wife, Groening once said, "She handles the business because I'm slow and naive when it comes to that."[99]

Another fan of Groening's outrageous strip was James L. Brooks, the creator of the television series *The Mary Tyler Moore Show* and *Taxi* and the director of several movies. In 1987, Brooks was producing the comedy television program *The Tracey Ullman Show* for the Fox network. Wanting to add short cartoon segments, known as bumpers, to the show, Brooks approached Groening with the idea of animating *Life in Hell*. Groening took on the assignment. But instead of bringing Binky, Sheba, and Bongo to the small screen, he introduced five new characters: Homer, Marge, Bart, Lisa, and Maggie Simpson.

The Simpsons

The first bumper featuring the Simpsons aired on September 8, 1987. Forty-eight more installments followed. Fans of the offbeat comedy show loved Groening's slightly twisted cartoon family. Sensing a potential hit, Fox commissioned Groening to produce thirteen half-hour episodes of *The Simpsons* with Brooks, Groening, and Sam Simon as executive producers.

The show was supposed to debut in the fall of 1989, but a problem arose. Some of the animators hired to produce the first episode had added their own gags to the program. Groening, Brooks, and Simon were horrified to find several tasteless jokes inserted into the final version of the first episode, including a scene in a television show the Simpson children are watching in which a bear cub rips the head off of an elf and drinks its blood. The producers who would later pride themselves on battling network censors pulled the plug on their own premiere episode. Instead of starting in the fall, the first episode of *The Simpsons* aired as a Christmas special in 1989, with the regular series beginning in January 1990.

The Simpsons immediately became the Fox network's highest-rated program. By 1998 the show had earned thirty Emmy nominations and won six Emmy Awards. Four of the Emmys awarded were for Outstanding Animated Program and two were for Outstanding Music and Lyrics. Two more Emmys were awarded to the show's actors for their Outstanding Voice-Over Performances.

America's favorite cartoon family, the Simpsons, includes (left to right) Maggie, Lisa, Bart, Marge, and Homer.

Even with such high critical praise, *The Simpsons* created an immediate controversy. Many parents found Bart Simpson to be a horrible role model for children. He talks back to teachers, lies to his parents, and enjoys spray-painting graffiti on buildings. Still a rebel at heart, Groening is unapologetic about his humor: "The secret thing I'm trying to do, behind entertainment, is to subvert. And if I can make myself and my friends laugh and can annoy the hell out of a political conservative, I feel like I've done my job."[100]

Denise Vitola, science fiction author, believes that Groening's satire serves a useful purpose:

> Cartoonists like Matt Groening are our world's most important resources, especially in this country. They thumb their noses at society. That's a very good thing to do on occasion because the rude gestures get our attention. And *The Simpsons* have definitely gotten our attention.[101]

What Makes the Show Work

Groening believes that one major factor in the series' amazing success is the music involved in the programs. Early on, he instinctively knew that music would enhance an emotional connection with viewers, so he worked hard to find just the right person to help structure the show's theme. Groening approached Danny Elfman, a musician he remembered from his time spent in Los Angeles. He had seen Elfman many times and had enjoyed hearing the musician at the Whisky-a-Go-Go, a club on the Sunset Strip in Hollywood.

> I gave Elfman what I called a "flavors" tape, featuring the kind of sound I wanted for *The Simpsons* theme. Elfman gave it a listen and said, "I know exactly what you're looking for." A month later we were recording the now-famous *The Simpsons* theme on the 20th Century-Fox lot with a huge orchestra. I think all the producers were a little nervous and fidgety about the untrendy audacity of the music. But then-executive producer James L. Brooks came in, listened a bit, then said, "My God! This is great!"[102]

The well-known theme was just the beginning for the music on *The Simpsons*. Since then, Alf Clausen has joined the musical team as a composer and songwriter. His contributions to the show have made a major impact. Each week Clausen puts together an average of thirty musical cues for a single episode, making *The Simpsons* a multitextured program. The program has even spawned two successful compact discs, *The Simpsons: Songs in the Key of Springfield* and *The Yellow Album*.

Because of the show's success, Groening has been able to snag major stars as guest voice performers. Movie stars such as Mel Gibson, Ron Howard, Helen Hunt, Danny DeVito, and Kathleen Turner have all offered their voice talents on *The Simpsons*. The successful cartoonist also feels that the controversy that surrounded *The Simpsons* in the beginning seasons has been overshadowed because of the show's respect for its audience.

> It really delivers the goods. It's a funny show. The characters are surprisingly likable, given how ugly they are. . . . People really appreciate not being condescended to. The history of TV has traditionally been not to do anything that would scandalize grandma or upset junior. Our solution on *The Simpsons* is to do jokes that people who have an education and some frame of reference can get. And the ones who don't, it doesn't matter, because we have Homer banging his head and saying "'D'oh!"[103]

Futurama

In March 1999 Groening took the talents that made his first animated series a hit to a new level. He created a young character named Fry and tossed him one-thousand years into the future.

Futurama drops Fry, a bored pizza delivery boy, into a new setting, but with a familiar job—delivering packages for Planet Express. Groening has also given Fry a couple of odd friends: Bender, a robot with a bad attitude, and Leela, the pilot who flies Fry and Bender on their delivery assignments. One reviewer critiquing the new series mentioned specific examples of Groening's comic creativity and stated that the show is true to the cartoonist's talent for contrasts:

> In *Futurama*, a midseason replacement . . . Groening transports his message a millennium into the future, to the *new* New York of the year 3000. Slyly piercing the hype and optimism that surround new technology, the show is populated by 20th-century celebrity talking heads in jars . . . while you sleep advertising, one-eyed aliens, jet powered scooters . . . and a corrupt megacorporation run by a despotic mom. . . . Like the rest of us, he's both fascinated and anxious about

the fast-forward, high tech, tool-laden world we're making—a keen ambivalence that makes *Futurama* a signature Groening 66 paradoxarama.[104]

In an interview with *TV Guide*, the cartoonist's childlike enthusiasm came through when comparing his first show featuring a semitraditional family with this new animated series that has nothing traditional in it at all:

The template for *The Simpsons* was a conventional 1950s sitcom, which we twisted around. . . . Most television does not reward viewers for paying attention. You've seen it once and that's often one time too many. On *Futurama* we're trying to make it so that you *can't* get everything in one viewing. . . . One of the great things about animation is that you can cram a lot more quotes and references and plot twists in a cartoon than in live action, and we've taken full advantage of that. This show is so jammed with visual jokes that we've even got an alien alphabet that we're not translating. We're going to allow our fans to try to figure out what those things say.[105]

A cel from Futurama *depicts the character Leela.*

Groening's passion for his work and his dedication to viewer intelligence have kept his cartoons fresh and popular. The extremely high number of *Futurama* viewers has proven that Groening's characters have been favorites among his fans for many years. One reviewer believes that although the new series is young, it promises to bring more character-driven, animated humor to television.

In a society where everyone's life is programmed, Groening's characters keep making trouble. "If there's an underlying message in this show," he says, "it's that the authorities don't always have your best interests in mind. No matter what they say."[106]

To help promote the release of the "Virtual Springfield" CD-ROM in 1997, Matt Groening poses for a photograph with his eight-year-old son, Will, inside a life-size replica of the Simpsons' home.

All three of Groening's successful cartoons have focused on bluntly criticizing any major government or organization. The political, religious, and cultural themes have caused controversy and created likable contrasts in his characters. Those realistic contrasts have continued to show up in Groening's new projects and have made him a prime-time political cartoonist. One recent comment in an article about cartoonists mentioned the appeal of Groening's contributions:

> If there is a future in American political cartooning, it may lie in illustrators from the thriving, once-underground "alternative" press. Perhaps the most successful is Matt Groening. Out of his strip *Life in Hell* came the cartoon on Fox TV, *The Simpsons.*[107]

Responses such as these far outnumber the few responses that have criticized the cartoonist for his rude and brazen material. Through it all, Groening has become a financial success as well as a noted influence on his audience. He even started his own comic-book publishing business in 1993 called the Bongo Comics Group. The comic books, which include "Simpsons Comics," "Bartman," "Radioactive Man," and "Itchy and Scratchy Comics," are spin-offs from *The Simpsons.*

People have always paid attention to the issues involved in Groening's work, but more than that, they have found comic relief in his satire. His comedy has provided a politically correct, but stifled, nation a voice of realism and release. And it has earned the boy who doodled in school an important role in modern cartooning and in society. As Groening once put it, "One of the great thrills of my life is that I now get paid for what I used to get sent to the principal's office for."[108]

CHAPTER 7

Scott Adams

Scott Adams, the creator of *Dilbert*, turned corporate offices upside down when he first introduced the nerdy character Dilbert in 1989. Ten years later, Adams has continued to skewer office politics and policies in the *Dilbert* comic strip, several *Dilbert* books, and an animated *Dilbert* television series. The strip alone appears in nineteen hundred newspapers in fifty-eight countries.

In each edition Adams helps his readers not take themselves—or their mighty bosses—too seriously. He and Dilbert have become heroes of the average corporate coworker, and they show no signs of slowing down their support system.

Child Cartoonist

Scott Adams was born on June 8, 1957, in Windham, New York, in the Catskill Mountains. His father, Paul, was a postal clerk and his mother, Virginia, was a homemaker and assembly-line worker. From as far back as he can remember, Adams says his mother encouraged him to be anything he wanted to be. She would have preferred her son trying to be president, but Adams always told her he wanted to be like Charles Schulz.

Throughout his childhood and school years, Adams loved to draw. When he was only eleven, he applied to the Famous Artists School, a correspondence school that taught art lessons through the mail instead of in a classroom. He filled out the questionnaire and in the space that asked, "Why would you like to be an artist?" Adams replied, "It could be a good job when I get older."[109]

Adams performed well on the artistic aptitude test and earned positive comments from the professional artist who judged his test. Unfortunately, Adams received a letter from the director of the school telling him that he was too young to be admitted into the program. The director's words, however, did encourage young Adams to keep working at his drawing skills.

> Thank you for completing this Talent Test and sending it to us for our comments. For a person of your age you did well with it. However, the Famous Artists Course for

Talented Young People is for students older than you. . . . We want everyone who takes our course to learn as much as he (or she) can from it. For this reason you should wait until you are twelve years old before you enroll. In the meantime, you can improve your ability by drawing and painting whenever you have the opportunity.[110]

Although Adams did not try again to enroll in the school, he did continue to draw every chance he had. After graduating from high school, Adams entered Hartwick College in Oneonta, New York. While attending college, he signed up for a drawing class. Unfortunately, his art skills didn't make much of an impression on his teacher, and Adams earned only a B-, the lowest

Dilbert creator Scott Adams holds up a drawing of his popular cartoon character.

grade among his fellow art students. Following that poor performance, he concentrated on studying for his degree in economics.

When he graduated from Hartwick, Adams moved to California, earning his masters degree from Berkeley in 1986. That same year Adams took a job as a technology worker for Pacific Bell's (PacBell) headquarters in northern California. During the next seven years, Adams found himself working a hectic job in the confines of a cubicle. He didn't especially like his job, but he chose to keep at it, hoping for better times ahead.

> I figured that if I worked hard and was smart, I could get promoted. It wasn't until I was well into it that I realized you also had to have good hair.[111]

Adams enjoyed poking fun at his own appearance, drawing doodles of a nerdy fellow with thick glasses and an even thicker middle who was kind of a universal reflection of Adams's life in the maze of corporate America. Before long, the potato-shaped techie with the pointy tie became a recurring character around the office. Adams says his coworkers liked the cartoon character so much that he decided to hold a "name-the-nerd" contest. The winning suggestion was "Dilbert."

With a real name, Dilbert was officially born. Adams knew the personality-challenged character had value. Dilbert would be the voice of common sense in an environment of cubicles—a physical world that Adams believed was designed to suppress worker creativity.

Dilbert would be the spokesman for every frustrated office worker lost in a big company with an inept boss. And if anyone knew about dim-witted bosses, it was Dilbert. His boss was notorious for barking out ridiculous orders to Dilbert and his coworkers, Wally and Alice.

> Boss: (to Dilbert, Wally, and Alice) In order to build team spirit I've decided you should have lunch together once a week. I won't be there myself because it would seriously cut into my free time. Besides, it's my job to motivate, not get bogged down in details.[112]

Adams knew there would be readers who would love a comic strip that blasted bad bosses. He believed he had enough economic sense to build reader loyalty and a small cartooning business, but first he needed to find *Dilbert* a home in the syndicates.

Becoming a Real Cartoonist

One way Adams chose to work on his goal of becoming a successful cartoonist was to spend time each day envisioning and affirming his desire:

> The basic idea is that 15 times a day you just write down your goal. Then you'll observe things happening that will make this objective more likely to materialize.[113]

Adams went a step further than simply writing down affirmations to make his dream of cartooning a reality. He also continued to draw and fine-tune his artwork. When he felt comfortable with the quality of the humor and the drawings, he then submitted sample comic strips to syndicates. Although he collected quite a few rejections, the one acceptance he did receive was priceless. United Media's United Feature Syndicate, the same syndicate that distributed his hero Charles Schulz and the *Peanuts* comic strip, offered him a contract.

Even with the acceptance and the contract, the comic strip *Dilbert* had a slow start. After a year of distribution, an average of only one hundred newspapers carried the strip. Adams studied the problem from his strong economic background and chose to do something daring.

In 1993 Scott Adams became the first cartoonist to list his e-mail address in his strip. He believed that an open line of communication would help him receive feedback from his audience. With that reader feedback he hoped to mold *Dilbert* into a comic strip that would appeal to more readers. His strategy worked.

E-mail messages began pouring into his computer. His fans told him exactly what they loved about the strip and what they didn't care for. Adams says it was this input that made the difference in *Dilbert*'s success:

Scott Adams poses in his office with a soft sculpture of Dilbert in 1996.

The business-oriented strips were being hung on walls, so I switched emphasis to 80-percent business and technology—and that's when the strip took off.[114]

Basically, Adams applied the fundamental principle of economics—which is to supply goods that the consumers want—to his new business and turned it into a phenomenal success. His ability to relate so well to the office environment has been a key to the success of *Dilbert*. His readers have shown Adams not only loyalty but an appreciation for his empathy of their daily plight.

In fact, Adams has caused the upper-level management of some companies to take notice of the subjects he attacks with humor. One company even has a "Dilbertization committee" that tries to find things that its employees do that might show up in a *Dilbert* cartoon and then get rid of those unproductive practices.

Guy Kawasaki, who works as a marketing expert for Apple Computer, believes *Dilbert* is the best example for showing the inner workings of big business—even when they aren't pretty: "There are only two kinds of companies: those that recognize they're just like *Dilbert*, and those that are just like *Dilbert* but don't know it."[115]

As Scott Adams's name became more popular and *Dilbert* cartoons became the new wallpaper for many cubicles, Adams still continued his job with PacBell. It wasn't until 1996, after his book *The Dilbert Principle* soared to number two on the *New York Times* best-seller list, that he and his bosses decided he should leave. As one reporter noted, the book hit a sore spot with Adams's supervisor:

> When Adams' *Dilbert Principle*, which holds that managers "were usually the people you missed least from the productive level," was published . . . it proved a turning point. Adams had a standing agreement that he would resign from PacBell whenever the public-relations value of having him no longer paid his way—and his boss took him up on it.[116]

As *Dilbert* rose to success, Adams added elements to the strip to lure more readers. Some of the additions were based on the e-mail messages he still received on a daily basis. For the dog lovers, he added power-hungry Dogbert, whose main goal is to conquer all humans. For cat lovers, he created Catbert, a director of human resources with a cat's indifference to the plight of employees.

When he built his own business, Adams tried to avoid the behaviors he lampooned in his strip. Adams considers his work a small business and has warmed to the idea of simplifying his life

to do only the cartooning. After all, as an entrepreneur, he is able to talk about his profitable one-man corporation and compare it to larger companies. This opportunity gave Adams a chance to continue taking shots at big business, which underscores the heart of the *Dilbert* strip:

> Small businesses don't have the luxury to absorb the same level of incompetence that big businesses do. If they try to enjoy that luxury, they cease to be small businesses and quickly become extinct businesses. In a big company, some people's entire jobs are to interfere with other people's jobs. For every person actually doing something, there's a person auditing their performance, monitoring quality control, and making sure they are not ordering pencils when they don't have the authority. Huge institutions have many people who do nothing but prevent other people from doing their jobs. So it's no surprise that small business is more efficient.[117]

Adams's outspoken observations of big business and its bumbling nature have helped him find publication for seventeen books. Unlike other cartoonists, some of Adams's books are more than compilations of his comic strip. Some, such as *The Dilbert Principle* and *The Dilbert Future*, have incorporated *Dilbert* cartoons with written satire, emphasizing Adams's biting views regarding big business.

In *The Dilbert Future*, Adams comments on the irony of the early 1980s when many people hoped that being employed by a large company meant job security. He believes that big business suffered most in the long run when it realized that the employees it laid off, a procedure known as downsizing, really were important to running a quality company.

> Working for a big company was a great deal until the nineties. If you could get hired, it was practically impossible to get fired. . . . Then the era of downsizing came. Employees were shoveled out the door faster than a pile of dead chipmunks at a cotillion. . . . They were capable of doing excellent work if anybody had thought to ask. Suddenly they were unemployed. Out of necessity, they reinvented themselves as "self-employed" people. . . . Time passed. Then a funny thing happened. Downsized companies discovered they couldn't run a multinational company with just a CEO and a Diversity Director. They needed employees.[118]

It is Adams's unending voice for the corporate little guy that surfaces over and over again in all formats of his humor. By 1999 Adams had taken that voice and crossed into animation, following in the footsteps of other influential cartoonists. The television series debuted with a strong following of viewers.

The advantage that Adams sees in the comic strip, as opposed to his books or the television series, is its convenience for the employees who often feel faceless in the large companies they work for. Scott Adams knows that his real "mission goal"—a term used in big companies to chart priorities—is to help employees make a statement in their companies. He believes that stupidities *Dilbert* exposes are truths that many employees wish they could force their bosses to see:

> It's a general truth that the more you know, the better the decisions you'll make. One thing managers don't know is what employees are thinking or how strongly they hold their opinions. There are obvious reasons why you don't tell your boss he's an idiot. And the *Dilbert* strip does tell bosses things, especially when an employee clips it out of the paper, pushes it under their door and runs away—which happens a lot.[119]

Even though Adams delivers these truths with such power that employees often clip his cartoons out of the paper and sneak them into their bosses' offices, he is slow to admit to all that he's done for people. In typical Dogbert fashion, he believes his job is still simply economics:

> I see myself as an entrepreneur who found a way to transfer wealth from other people to himself. All the other things people say about me—"He's changing how people

89

manage"—happen externally to me. That's not my goal. I'm not trying to encourage it. I can't stop it, and if other people are saying it's happening, that's fine. Basically, I'm simply a small-business owner.[120]

Adams is pleased that his work has opened some eyes and has helped bring about changes in some workplaces. But what he really found out by drawing a daily comic strip—just as his favorite cartoonist, Charles Schulz, has done for over fifty years—is exactly what he guessed when he was eleven: Being an artist really is a good job now that he's older.

NOTES

Chapter 1: The History of Cartooning

1. Syd Hoff, *Editorial and Political Cartooning*. New York: Stravon Educational Press, 1976, pp. 24–25.
2. Hoff, *Editorial and Political Cartooning*, p. 31.
3. David Relin, "The President Maker," *Scholastic Update*, October 4, 1996, p. 18.
4. Robert C. Harvey, *The Art of the Funnies: An Aesthetic History*. Jackson: University of Mississippi Press, 1994, p. 4.
5. Harvey, *The Art of the Funnies*, p. 8.
6. Harvey, *The Art of the Funnies*, p. 7.
7. Harvey, *The Art of the Funnies*, p. 72.
8. Adam Philips and Benjamin Svetkey, "Funny Business," *EW Magazine Online*, October 5, 1990, p. 1. www.etweekly.com.

Chapter 2: Charles Schulz

9. "About Charles Schulz," The Official Peanuts Home Page, March 31, 1999, p. 1. www.unitedmedia.com/comics/peanuts/index. html.
10. Quoted in Rheta G. Johnson, *Good Grief: The Story of Charles M. Schulz*. New York: Pharos Books, 1989, p. 17.
11. Quoted in Gaye LeBaron, "Drawn to His Trade," *Press Democrat On-Line*, November 23, 1997, p. 2. www.pressdemo.com.
12. Quoted in Johnson, *Good Grief*, p. 18.
13. Quoted in Johnson, *Good Grief*, p. 43.
14. Quoted in Johnson, *Good Grief*, p. 42.
15. Johnson, *Good Grief*, pp. 42–43.
16. Quoted in Johnson, *Good Grief*, p. 90.
17. Harvey, *The Art of the Funnies*, p. 211.
18. Quoted in Rich Marschall and Gary Groth, "Charles Schulz Interview," *Nemo 31*, January 1992, p. 12.
19. Quoted in Harvey, *The Art of the Funnies*, p. 215.
20. Harvey, *The Art of the Funnies*, p. 216.
21. Quoted in Harvey, *The Art of the Funnies*, p. 217.

22. Quoted in Harvey, *The Art of the Funnies*, p. 217.

23. Harvey, *The Art of the Funnies*, p. 216.

24. Quoted in Johnson, *Good Grief*, p. 27.

25. Quoted in Johnson, *Good Grief*, p. 28.

26. Quoted in Shel Dorf, "The Fantasy Makers: Interview with Mort Walker," *Buyer's Guide*, n.d., n.p.

27. Quoted in Elaine Scott, *Funny Papers*. New York: Morrow Junior Books, 1993, p. 19.

28. Quoted in Jenifer Hanrahan, "Rats! Ailing Schulz to Retire," *San Diego Union-Tribune*, December 15, 1999, p. A1.

Chapter 3: Chuck Jones

29. Quoted in Judith Graham, ed., *Current Biography Yearbook 1996*. New York: H. W. Wilson, 1996, p. 235.

30. Quoted in Graham, *Current Biography Yearbook 1996*, p. 235.

31. Chuck Jones, *Chuck Amuck: The Life and Times of an Animated Cartoonist*. New York: Farrar Straus Giroux, 1989, p. 49.

32. Jones, *Chuck Amuck*, p. 50.

33. Jones, *Chuck Amuck*, p. 15.

34. Jones, *Chuck Amuck*, p. 20.

35. "Chuck Jones, Animation Pioneer," *The Hall of Arts*, March 31, 1999, p. 2. www.achievement.org/autodoc/page/jon1bio-1.

36. Jones, *Chuck Amuck*, p. 53.

37. Richard Corliss, "Cartoons Are No Laughing Matter," *Time*, May 12, 1997, p. 80.

38. Quoted in Graham, *Current Biography Yearbook 1996*, p. 236.

39. Jones, *Chuck Amuck*, p. 261.

40. Jones, *Chuck Amuck*, p. 261.

41. Quoted in Graham, *Current Biography Yearbook 1996*, p. 237.

42. Jones, *Chuck Amuck*, p. 235.

43. Lloyd Rose, "Our Greatest Invisible Actor," *Atlantic*, December 1984, pp. 124–25.

44. Quoted in Graham, *Current Biography Yearbook 1996*, p. 239.

45. Quoted in Nita G. Bateman, "Chuck Jones: Producer, Director, Writer," *Collecting Online*, March 31, 1999, p. 1.

Chapter 4: Garry Trudeau

46. Quoted in Garry Trudeau, *Flashbacks: Twenty-Five Years of Doonesbury*. Kansas City: Andrews and McMeel, 1995, p. 12.

47. Quoted in Harvey, *The Art of the Funnies*, p. 228.

48. Trudeau, *Flashbacks*, p. 11.

49. Quoted in Trudeau, *Flashbacks*, p. 10.

50. Nora Ephron, Afterword to *Joanie*. New York: Sheed and Ward, 1974, p. 94.

51. Garry Trudeau, *The People's* Doonesbury. New York: Holt, Rinehart, and Winston, 1981, p. 3.

52. Quoted in Trudeau, *Flashbacks*, p. 32.

53. Quoted in Charles Moritz, ed., *Current Biography Yearbook 1975*. New York: H. W. Wilson, 1975, p. 421.

54. Trudeau, *Flashbacks*, p. 37.

55. Trudeau, *Flashbacks*, p. 57.

56. Allan Parachini, "Social Protest Hits the Comic Pages," *Columbia Journalism Review*, November/December 1974, p. 6.

57. Quoted in Johnson, *Good Grief*, p. 97.

58. Harvey, *The Art of the Funnies*, p. 230.

59. Harvey, *The Art of the Funnies*, p. 229.

60. Harvey, *The Art of the Funnies*, p. 230.

61. Harvey, *The Art of the Funnies*, p. 230.

62. Trudeau, *Flashbacks*, p. 201.

63. Quoted in Greg Lucas, "Lungren Isn't Laughing," *San Francisco Chronicle*, October 2, 1996, p. A1.

64. Quoted in Simeon Leake, "The *Doonesbury* Story," *The People's* Doonesbury@AMAZON.COM, June 19, 1999, p. 1. www.amazon.com/exec/obidos/subst/promotions/doonesbury.

Chapter 5: Cathy Guisewite

65. Cathy Guisewite, "Cathy's Original Submissions," *Universal New Media*, June 9, 1999, p.1. www.uexpress.com/ups/comics/ca/html/submission.html.

66. Quoted in Charles Moritz, ed., *Current Biography Yearbook 1989*. New York: H. W. Wilson, 1989, p. 225.

67. Quoted in Moritz, *Current Biography Yearbook 1989*, p. 224.

68. Quoted in Mary James, "Cathy and Her Mom," *Woman's Day,* July 13, 1982, p. 96.

69. Quoted in Raymond Serafin, "Cathy in Real Life," *Advertising Age*, October 17, 1985, p. 5.

70. Quoted in Janice Harayda, "Talking with . . . Cathy Guisewite," *Glamour*, July 1978, p. 84.

71. Cathy Guisewite, "Quotables," 1st *Person*, June 9, 1999, p. 1. www.sunherald.com/1pguise/html/1d.htm.

72. Quoted in Harayda, "Talking with . . . Cathy Guisewite," p. 88.

73. Cathy Guisewite, International Museum of Cartoonists biographical note, 1997.

74. Quoted in Cork Millner, "Cathy: How Cartoonist Cathy Guisewite Makes Us Laugh at Life's Little Frustrations," *Seventeen*, May 1983, p. 42.

75. Quoted in Cathy Guisewite, *Another Saturday Night of Wild and Reckless Abandon.* Kansas City: Andrews and McMeel, 1982, inside cover.

76. Harvey, *The Art of the Funnies*, p. 239.

77. Quoted in Moritz, *Current Biography Yearbook 1989*, p. 225.

78. Moritz, *Current Biography Yearbook 1989*, p. 225.

79. Harvey, *The Art of the Funnies*, p. 239.

80. Guisewite, "Quotables," p. 1.

81. Guisewite, "Quotables," pp. 1–2.

82. Cathy Guisewite, *Why Do the Right Words Always Come Out of the Wrong Mouth?* Kansas City: Andrews and McMeel, 1988, p. 105.

83. Quoted in Carol Saline and Sharon J. Wolmuth, *Mothers and Daughters.* New York: Doubleday, 1997, p. 12.

84. Cathy Guisewite, Cathy *Twentieth Anniversary Collection.* Kansas City: Andrews and McMeel, 1996, p. 29.

85. Guisewite, *Why Do the Right Words Always Come Out of the Wrong Mouth?* p. 85.

86. Quoted in Charlotte Larvala, "Wedding Bells for Cathy," *Good Housekeeping,* November 1997, p. 27.

87. Guisewite, Cathy *Twentieth Anniversary Collection*, p. 111.

Chapter 6: Matt Groening

88. Quoted in Neil Tesser, "Twenty Questions: Matt Groening," *Playboy*, July 1990, p. 131.

89. Quoted in Kim Thompson, "Matt Groening," in Gary Groth and Robert Fiore, *The New Comics*. New York: Berkley Books, 1988, p. 240.

90. Quoted in Thompson, "Matt Groening," p. 238.

91. Quoted in Charles Moritz, ed., *Current Biography Yearbook 1989*. New York: H. W. Wilson, 1989, p. 286.

92. Quoted in Joe Morgenstern, "Bart Simpson's Real Father," *Los Angeles Times Magazine*, April 29, 1990, p. 17.

93. Quoted in Sean Elder, "Is TV the Coolest Invention Ever Invented?" *Mother Jones*, December 1989, p. 31.

94. Quoted in Tesser, "Twenty Questions: Matt Groening," p. 136.

95. Quoted in Tish Hamilton, "The Cartoon Hell of Matt Groening," *Rolling Stone*, September 22, 1988, p. 113.

96. Quoted in Shannon Picken, "The Simpsons Folder," *Fox News*, April 1, 1999, p. 1. www.fox.com.

97. Quoted in Hamilton, "The Cartoon Hell of Matt Groening," p. 113.

98. Richard Harrington, "Drawing on the Humor in Life's Little Horrors," *Washington Post*, December 18, 1988, p. F16.

99. Quoted in Tesser, "Twenty Questions: Matt Groening," p. 136.

100. Quoted in Hamilton, "The Cartoon Hell of Matt Groening," p. 82.

101. Denise Vitola, interview with the author, Joshua, TX, May 19, 1999.

102. Matt Groening, "The Musical Prehistory of *The Simpsons*," *Liner Notes*, April 1, 1999, p. 2. www.fox.com.

103. Matt Groening, "Q & A with Matt Groening," *E! Online— The Hot Spot*, April 1, 1999, pp. 2–3. www.eonline.com.

104. Kevin Kelly, "One-Eyed Aliens! Suicide Booths! Mom's Old-Fashioned Robot Oil!" *Wired*, February 1999, pp. 1–2. www.wired.com/wired/archive/7.02/futurama.html.

105. Quoted in Joe Rhodes, "Future Mock," *TV Guide*, March 25, 1998, pull-out section.

106. Rhodes, "Future Mock," pull-out section.

107. Quoted in *Economist*, "Moreover," November 2, 1996, p. 84.

108. Quoted in Tesser, "Twenty Questions: Matt Groening," p. 136.

Chapter 7: Scott Adams

109. Scott Adams, "Birth of a Cartoonist," *Dilbert Zone*, March 31, 1999, p. 2. www.unitedmedia.com/comic/dilbert/scott/birth/birth03.html.

110. Quoted in Adams, "Birth of a Cartoonist," p. 2.

111. Quoted in Steven Levy, "The View from Dilbert's Cubicle," *Reader's Digest*, July 1997, p. 59.

112. Scott Adams, *Still Pumped from Using the Mouse*. Kansas City: Andrews and McMeel, 1996, p. 34.

113. Quoted in Levy, "The View from Dilbert's Cubicle," pp. 59–60.

114. Quoted in Levy, "The View from Dilbert's Cubicle," p. 60.

115. Quoted in Levy, "The View from Dilbert's Cubicle," p. 56.

116. Janet Cawley and Gabrielle Saveri, "Corporate Raider," *People*, June 3, 1996, p. 98.

117. Quoted in Robert McGarvey, "The *Adams* Principle," *Entrepreneur*, September 1997, p. 118.

118. Scott Adams, *The Dilbert Future*. New York: HarperCollins, 1997, pp. 126–27.

119. Quoted in McGarvey, "The *Adams* Principle," pp. 122–23.

120. Quoted in McGarvey, "The *Adams* Principle," p. 123.

FOR FURTHER READING

Scott McCloud, *Understanding Comics: The Invisible Art.* Northampton, MA: Tundra, 1993. McCloud traces the development of sequential art from ancient Egypt to the present in exhaustive detail. The book includes valuable discussions of how comics are composed, how they are read, and how they are understood.

Judith O'Sullivan, *The Great American Comic Strip: One Hundred Years of Comic Art.* Boston: Little, Brown, 1990. Richly illustrated with hundreds of vintage cartoons in both black and white and color, this book offers a concise survey of the modern comic strip. The book includes a valuable "Who's who of the comic strip" that profiles more than 250 cartoonists.

Trina Robbins, *A Century of Woman Cartoonists.* Northampton, MA: Kitchen Sink Press, 1993. Robbins examines the contribution of women to the evolution of an art form traditionally dominated by men.

Elaine Scott, *Funny Papers.* New York: Morrow Junior Books, 1993. Richy illustrated with full-size comic strips as well as black-and-white photographs by Margaret Miller, *Funny Papers* takes a behind-the-scenes look at how comic strips are created, from inspiration to final production.

Charles Solomon, *The History of Animation.* New York: Wings Books, 1989, 1994. A valuable overview of the development of moving cartoons.

Harvey Weiss, *Cartoons and Cartooning.* Boston: Houghton Mifflin, 1990. An artist, illustrator, and professor of art history, Weiss brings the insight of a practitioner to this brief but informative analysis of the art form. Illustrated with a wider-than-usual selection of cartooning styles, the book even includes a brief section on how to draw cartoons.

WORKS CONSULTED

Books

Scott Adams, *The Dilbert Future*. New York: HarperCollins, 1997. Text and cartoons that give readers Adams's views of what large corporations will be like in the future.

Scott Adams, *Still Pumped from Using the Mouse*. Kansas City: Andrews and McMeel, 1996. Collection of *Dilbert* comic strips.

Nora Ephron, Afterword to *Joanie*. New York: Sheed and Ward, 1974.

Randy Glasbergen, *How to Be a Successful Cartoonist*. Cincinnati: F & W Publications, 1996. Comprehensive look at the steps necessary to become a cartoonist; profiles of major and minor cartoonists plus bits of cartoonist history are also included.

Judith Graham, ed., *Current Biography Yearbook 1996*. New York: H. W. Wilson, 1996. Includes brief profiles of people who rose to prominence in 1996. Biographical sketches are supported with numerous quotes. Each entry concludes with a short bibliography.

Gary Groth and Robert Fiore, *The New Comics*. New York: Berkley Books, 1988. Compilation of interviews with adult and underground cartoonists who have made an impact in that industry; also includes definitions of "pulp," "fanzine," and "graphic" novels.

Cathy Guisewite, *Another Saturday Night of Wild and Reckless Abandon*. Kansas City: Andrews and McMeel, 1982. Collection of *Cathy* comic strips.

Cathy Guisewite, *Cathy Twentieth Anniversary Collection*. Kansas City: Andrews and McMeel, 1996. Collection of Guisewite's favorite strips and commentary from the cartoonist.

Cathy Guisewite, *Why Do the Right Words Always Come Out of the Wrong Mouth?* Kansas City: Andrews and McMeel, 1988. Collection of *Cathy* comic strips.

Robert C. Harvey, *The Art of the Funnies: An Aesthetic History*. Jackson: University of Mississippi Press, 1994. Possibly the most comprehensive study of the actual artwork behind the wit and satire of cartoonists throughout history.

Syd Hoff, *Editorial and Political Cartooning*. New York: Stravon Educational Press, 1976. A rich resource full of historical asides to add depth to the cartoonists and cartoons highlighted from the beginning of editorial cartooning.

Rheta G. Johnson, *Good Grief: The Story of Charles M. Schulz.* New York: Pharos Books, 1989. Authorized biography that depicts Schulz's life in a thorough and engaging text; also includes samples of his early work.

Chuck Jones, *Chuck Amuck: The Life and Times of an Animated Cartoonist.* New York: Farrar Straus Giroux, 1989. A fun and detailed autobiography that tells the story of one of the first animation cartoonists and also the history of animation.

Lee Mendelson, *Happy Birthday, Charlie Brown.* New York: Random House, 1979. Written by Schulz's film partner, this book offers highlights of the first thirty years of the *Peanuts* comic strip, as well as the films, television shows, and awards that *Peanuts* and Schulz have won.

Charles Moritz, ed., *Current Biography Yearbook 1975.* New York: H. W. Wilson, 1975. Includes brief profiles of people who rose to prominence in 1975. Biographical sketches are supported with numerous quotes. Each entry concludes with a short bibliography.

Charles Moritz, ed., *Current Biography Yearbook 1989.* New York: H. W. Wilson, 1989. Includes brief profiles of people who rose to prominence in 1989. Biographical sketches are supported with numerous quotes. Each entry concludes with a short bibliography.

Carol Saline and Sharon J. Wolmuth, *Mothers and Daughters.* New York: Doubleday, 1997. The authors of *Sisters* present photographs and essays that explore the intimate connection shared by mothers and daughters. Some of the subjects, such as Cindy Crawford, Margaret Atwood, and Jamie Lee Curtis, are famous, while others are not.

Garry Trudeau, *Flashbacks: Twenty-Five Years of* Doonesbury. Kansas City: Andrews and McMeel, 1995. A compilation of strips that show the major issues Trudeau has tackled through the first twenty-five years of *Doonesbury*; includes quotes from some of the people who know the cartoonist and some of the people who have been featured in his strips.

Garry Trudeau, *The People's* Doonesbury. New York: Holt, Rinehart, and Winston, 1981. Collection of *Doonesbury* comic strips.

Periodicals

Nita G. Bateman, "Chuck Jones: Producer, Director, Writer," *Collecting Online*, March 31, 1999.

Janet Cawley and Gabrielle Saveri, "Corporate Raider," *People*, June 3, 1996.

Richard Corliss, "Cartoons Are No Laughing Matter," *Time*, May 12, 1997.

Shel Dorf, "The Fantasy Makers: Interview with Mort Walker," *Buyer's Guide*, n.d., n.p.

Economist, "Moreover," November 2, 1996.

Sean Elder, "Is TV the Coolest Invention Ever Invented?" *Mother Jones*, December 1989.

Tish Hamilton, "The Cartoon Hell of Matt Groening," *Rolling Stone*, September 22, 1988.

Jenifer Hanrahan, "Rats! Ailing Schulz to Retire," *San Diego Union-Tribune*, December 15, 1999.

Janice Harayda, "Talking with . . . Cathy Guisewite," *Glamour*, July 1978.

Richard Harrington, "Drawing on the Humor in Life's Little Horrors," *Washington Post*, December 18, 1988.

Mary James, "Cathy and Her Mom," *Woman's Day*, July 13, 1982.

Charlotte Larvala, "Wedding Bells for Cathy," *Good Housekeeping*, November 1997.

Steven Levy, "The View from Dilbert's Cubicle," *Reader's Digest*, July 1997.

Greg Lucas, "Lungren Isn't Laughing," *San Francisco Chronicle*, October 2, 1996.

Rich Marschall and Gary Groth, "Charles Schulz Interview," *Nemo 31*, January 1992.

Robert McGarvey, "The *Adams* Principle," *Entrepreneur*, September 1997.

Cork Millner, "Cathy: How Cartoonist Cathy Guisewite Makes Us Laugh at Life's Little Frustrations," *Seventeen*, May 1983.

Joe Morgenstern, "Bart Simpson's Real Father," *Los Angeles Times Magazine*, April 29, 1990.

Allan Parachini, "Social Protest Hits the Comic Pages," *Columbia Journalism Review*, November/December 1974.

David Relin, "The President Maker," *Scholastic Update*, October 4, 1996.

Joe Rhodes, "Future Mock," *TV Guide*, March 25, 1998.

Lloyd Rose, "Our Greatest Invisible Actor," *Atlantic*, December 1984.

Raymond Serafin, "Cathy in Real Life," *Advertising Age*, October 17, 1985.

Neil Tesser, "Twenty Questions: Matt Groening," *Playboy*, July 1990.

Internet Sources

"About Charles Schulz," The Official Peanuts Home Page, March 31, 1999. www.unitedmedia.com/comics/peanuts/index.html.

Scott Adams, "Birth of a Cartoonist," *Dilbert Zone*, March 31, 1999. www.unitedmedia.com/comic/dilbert/scott/birth/birth03.html.

"Chuck Jones, Animation Pioneer," *The Hall of Arts*, March 31, 1999. www.achievement.org/autodoc/page/jon1bio-1.

Matt Groening, "The Musical Prehistory of *The Simpsons*," *Liner Notes*, April 1, 1999. www.fox.com.

Matt Groening, "Q & A with Matt Groening," *E! Online—The Hot Spot*, April 1, 1999. www.eonline.com.

Cathy Guisewite, "Cathy's Original Submissions," *Universal New Media*, June 9, 1999. www.uexpress.com/ups/comics/ca/html/submission.html.

Cathy Guisewite, "Quotables," *1st Person*, June 9, 1999. www.sunherald.com/1pguise/html/1d.htm.

Kevin Kelly, "One-Eyed Aliens! Suicide Booths! Mom's Old-Fashioned Robot Oil!" *Wired*, February 1999. www.wired.com/wired/archive/7.02/futurama.html.

Simeon Leake, "The *Doonesbury* Story," *The People's* Doonesbury@AMAZON.COM, June 19, 1999. www.amazon.com/exec/obidos/subst/promotions/doonesbury.

Gaye LeBaron, "Drawn to His Trade," *Press Democrat On-Line*, November 23, 1997. www.pressdemo.com.

Adam Philips and Benjamin Svetkey, "Funny Business," *EW Magazine Online*, October 5, 1990. www.etweekly.com.

Shannon Picken, "The Simpsons Folder," *Fox News*, April 1, 1999. www.fox.com.

INDEX

PICTURE CREDITS

ABOUT THE AUTHORS

A widely published poet and playwright, Bradley Steffens is the author of twelve books and coauthor of three more. He lives in Poway, California.

Robyn Weaver is a writer, editor, and continuing education instructor at Texas Christian University. Other books Weaver has written for Lucent include biographies of John Grisham and Alexander Graham Bell.